Bargain Chic

BARGAIN
Chic

by **Roberta Plutzik**

Lyle Stuart Inc.   Secaucus, New Jersey

Published by Lyle Stuart Inc.
120 Enterprise Ave., Secaucus, N.J. 07094
In Canada: Musson Book Company
A division of General Publishing Co. Limited.
Don Mills, Ontario

Queries regarding rights and permissions should be
addressed to: Lyle Stuart, 120 Enterprise Avenue,
Secaucus, N.J. 07094

Manufactured in the United States of America

Library of Congress Cataloging-in-Publication Data

Plutzik, Roberta.
    Bargain chic.

    1. Shopping—United States—Directories.
2. Clothing trade—United States—Directories.   I. Title.
TX335.P58   1985   646.3   85-14870
ISBN 0-8184-0383-7 (pbk.)

For Emmanuel and Estelle Plutzik

Acknowledgments

The best bargain hunters are sharers, people who can't wait to clue you into a good deal. I'm indebted to those who participated in the enjoyable "Bargain Roundtables" that provided the human foundation for this book: Frances Payne, Ann Forster, Robert Smolkin, Jeff Briggs, Amelia White, Neil Baldwin, Maria Laghi, Deborah Sue Plutzik, and the many other shoppers who spoke "off the cuff" to me.

My gratitude to more than two dozen newspaper fashion and lifestyle editors and reporters who offered their suggestions for the Bargain Resource Guide at the end of the book, and to Lisa Schwartz Schneider, who researched this section with sensitivity and care. I thank Iris Ellis of SOS, Inc., and her assistant, Kay Martin, for providing the outlet center listings, and for Iris's incisive comments on the bargain shopping life.

My appreciation, also, to two fine photographers and good friends, Ebet Roberts and Joan Tedeschi, who gave their time and creativity to this book on such short notice, and to Tara McCarron and Stanton Marchbanks, who are pictured on the jacket cover; to my brother, Jonathan Plutzik, for use of his "studio"; to my mother, Tanya Plutzik, for teaching me the highways and byways of bargain hunting *and* looking swell; and, again, to my sister, Deborah, for her chapter research, support, stories and ideas, as well as for all the outfits she bought me on sale through the years.

I appreciate the enthusiasm of the retailers and garment business specialists who on an off the record gave me first-hand information on how the business works today. Those who agreed to be mentioned are Leonard Atkin of NBO, Howard Eilenberg of Frederick Atkins, Monroe Milstein of Burlington Coat Factory, Andrea Rosen and Jill Salis of the Footwear Council, Mike Green of April-Marcus, Michael Merns of Merns, Kathy Lewson and Karen Glance of Boltons, Maria Mercado of Pappagallo, Clara Hancox of the *Daily News Record*, Alice Meyer, Diane Kaiser, Annette Swanberg, Viki King, Patricia Scotto. I also thank Dr. Herbert Freudenberger; Dr. Edward Christophersen; Jean Seligmann; Kimberly Hollifield; and the library staff at the Fashion Institute of Technology; and Lyle Stuart, Carole Livingston Stuart and Tom Roberts for their support and enthusiasm for this project.

Contents

9

"I always wear *something* that costs 10 cents."
—Viki King, West Coast Bargain Hunter, 1985

"The girls at exercise class were agog when they saw my pinkish-brownish-grayish twisted yarn tweed straight skirt with the 40s-Roz-Russell-style kickpleats.

" 'You're in luck,' I told them. 'I got this heavenly item at [store name]...and they're having a big sale. Prices, it is rumored, are so low they may actually *pay you* to buy the clothes. And bring a date—plenty of men's things, too...' Shreiking ensued, and everyone ran to grab a pen for details."
—Cynthia Heimel, *The Village Voice*, New York, 1985

Introduction: Up the Down Escalator

There it was. The $2.99 rack outside "Designer Fashions," a nondescript shop run by a man with good wholesale fashion connections who probably once worked in the garment district of Manhattan, and his solemn son. The name on the front had all but faded away, but this little store, on a downtown Brooklyn side street better known for burger joints, called out to me with the sweet sound of B-A-R-G-A-I-N-S. Indeed, on the ramshackle $2.99 rack (two for $5), a sky blue ultra-suede coat called out to me softly.

My built-in bargain bleepers began to flicker and as I came closer to the coat they brightened to a steady gleam. A silent sale shout rose within me as I brushed up against it and clutched the price tag. I quickly realized it was sample, lacking only buttons and belt.

I imagined the original cost—somewhere between $300 and $400, perhaps?—and what it would take to resurrect this catch into an utterly timeless addition to my wardrobe. The challenge stirred my bargain-hungry bones. I plunked down $2.99 plus tax, feeling as if I were about to make off with the crown jewels, only everybody else thought they were plastic. The solemn son remained poker-faced as he stuffed my precious find in a plain brown paper bag and unceremoniously stapled it shut. I scurried out of "Designer Fashions," a cockeyed grin on my face, my little heart racing to the tune of "Oh, What a Beautiful Morning." And it was.

The sun broke through the clouds as I floated down the block. Yes, I was in the throes of a bargain frenzy, which some of us believe is almost as much fun as sex. I took the coat directly to the cleaners. For $7.50, it looked like new. A fashion-buyer friend appraised my blue beauty. When I had it on, it made me feel like Lauren Bacall. Just as I thought, this was a $350 item that had, through what must have been several flukes, lost a few zeroes.

I was up to the challenge of restoration. I found a belt for $5—and just the right hue. Matching blue snaps cost 79 cents. I don't wear my ultra-suede fall/spring coat very often— but when I need it, it's there. As I put it on, aside from recalling the thrill of it's capture, I look and feel as if I were independently wealthy, lived on Madison Avenue, and regularly bought $350 coats. But the best part was the real cost to me—count it up— $16.28 (plus tax). As the proprietors of "Designer Fashions" so aptly put it about their best buys, "a steal." But nobody goes to prison for such a theft; quite the opposite.

Keeping it a secret is the real crime. There are enough bargains around for all of us. You just have to be smart enough to find them.

I relate this story of ultra suede, as I will many others about the joy of fashion bargain hunting, because for me and count-less other well-dressed individuals, the key to looking good is paying less. Far from being the neurotics they were once considered by the snooty pay-more-to-feel-better crowd, fash-ion bargain hunters of both sexes have now been vindicated by trends in retailing which have led to more terrific buys in more places, including my quaint Brooklyn hole-in-the-wall. Oh yes, my friend got an excellent maroon suede blazer there, for $35—a bargain for which she bargained another $5 off—and I've returned to pick up Giorgio Sant'Angelo blouses for ap-proximately 25 percent of their usual retail cost, as well as unlabeled gems on the famous $2.99 rack.

This book is for two kinds of people—those with a natural gift for fashion bargains who want to increase their skills even more; and others who have not bargain-hunted regularly with success in the past, but understand that they have been missing out. It's almost impossible today not to notice sales—store windows are plastered with advertisements for them every week of the year. But what to buy—when? Who to trust? And how not to sacrifice fashion in quest of frugality?

Follow me up the down escalator, toward the educated consumer's best revenge—the below-wholesale-cost bargain. Your wardrobe, your bank account and your self-image will never be the same.

CHAPTER 1

Style—Anything Goes

"When you go into a store, pick out something you like. It doesn't matter if it's 'two-years-ago' antique, or now—it's what appeals to you."
—Perry Ellis

Once upon a time, standards of dress were dictated by a country's monarchy, sometimes by decree. You wore what you were told, depending on who you were in society.

Today, while standards of "proper" dress do remain—punk-style shaved heads are *never* seen in the banking world—nobody faces punishment if, after hours, a business suit is replaced by jeans and a sweatshirt. Many of us have several roles—worker, spouse, friend, child, parent—and clothes help us define those often abrupt shifts we take in the course of a day or week.

Looking good—through fitness regimens and greater awareness of the importance of apparel—is no less than a national mania. But many of us are in such a hurry to "do" and "be" all we can, that we either don't have much time to shop effectively, or we haven't sufficient financial resources—or both. We're also constricted by outdated notions of what real style is. Add to these antiquated notions and economic considerations some longstanding myths about fashion bargain hunting.

But have you noticed? Though the changes that give fashion its very reason for being continue to evolve with each new season, fashion commentators and designers—a modern fashion monarchy—no longer tell us how to dress.

This marvelous freedom to respond and adapt to fashion innovations if and when they suit us is both exciting and just a little frightening. The work of top fashion designers can be helpful as we search for who we really are and how we really want to look. Forging a personal style, designers now insist, is what each of us must aspire to in this "anything goes" culture.

The new challenge is not to copy the king, but to create a consciousness of *who we are* as individuals at the same time that we're deciphering the crosswinds of fashion change. Fashion designers, in fact, are telling us that the more individualistic we are, the more innately stylish we may become.

The almost total freedom we have to dress as we see fit, to weigh sublime as well as ridiculous changes in fashion that take place from season to season, makes the great American pastime—shopping—a more liberated pursuit than ever before, for both sexes.

Smart shopping is striving both to imitate what we see out there on society's fashion leaders and to announce our own individuality—the personal flair that counts.

In a recent survey of 13,000 *Glamour* magazine readers, 95 percent said they had changed the way they dress in the last five years. More than half of them felt they were more "creative" now than ever before. Yet almost three-quarters of the respondents said their budgets were too slight for the quality clothing they wanted.

And that's very good news for the *bargain chic* philosophy, where, with a combination of canny consumerism and fashion risk-taking, a timeless wardrobe can be built on a modest budget.

***

A few years ago, the word *bargain* suggested cheap, miserable, cast-off merchandise that nobody else wanted. It was

You like hats? Pant suits? Even if "name" designers aren't showing them this season, the new "anything goes" fashion philosophy, espoused by industry types as well as real people, means wearing what's flattering to you. (Photo by Joan Tedeschi)

necessarily out of date, out of fashion and out of style. And you can't get much more *out* than that!

Bargain hunters from way back will protest this bad rap as undeserved. Sales and wonderful buys have always been available to those who cared to find them. But it was also true that due to *the way the retail apparel industry worked*, bargains were more unusual and more difficult to find. In the old days, for every bargain there was a season.

Today, every day, there are bargains galore to pluck off the blossoming bargain tree. Some of us are up there, with ladders, harvesting the goodies. Others stand back, doubtful of the possibilities. While skepticism is only natural, the ranks of *bargain chic* believers nevertheless grow as men and women acquire artful shopping techniques and the self-confidence that leads to solid personal fashion statements.

Many books have been written to show us how to present ourselves stylishly by adhering to one school of fashion or another.

The aim of this book is to show you how to shop smart—so smart that you will *always* look your best. At its most rewarding, shopping the *bargain chic* way will enhance your taste, not sacrifice it. As you develop bargain hunting skills, you will be writing your own dress-for-success bible.

Its chief commandment will be: *Thou shalt not spend more than half the original price of any garment, and usually much less—without sacrificing quality or self-image.*

The New Bargain Hunters

If they once were penny pinchers clutching change purses for dear life, they now are leaders in our cultures. A *Los Angeles Times* survey of Southern California shoppers discovered that it's this nation's upscale "achievers" —some 20 percent of the population—as well as the "socially conscious" and individualistic "I-am-me" types among us who prefer shopping at discounted prices.

The new bargain hunters are upscale achievers, socially conscious and strongly individualistic. And being dressed head-to-toe in markdowns makes them smile. (Photo by Joan Tedeschi)

Achievers, the study notes, "are defenders of the economic status quo and purchasers of top brands, top services and the newest and best of everything" —but at the price *they* want to pay. Socially conscious shoppers are "activistic, impassioned and knowledgeable"; the "I-am-me" breed are strongly individualistic, artistic and eager for "involvement and experience" in life. Only the survey's so-called "Belongers" haven't hopped on the bargain bandwagon.

Those who have, discover what Iris Ellis, editor of the nationwide *SOS Save on Shopping Directory,* has been saying for years: "Just because it's cheap doesn't mean it isn't perfect. People who are naturally more clever, who are able to locate the bargains, really enjoy them, and not just because they look good. Bargain hunters definitely feel as if they've 'won the game,' that they're undercover agents who've made their move at the right time and achieved something special by doing it."

Recognizing the Important Difference Between Style and Fashion

Occasionally, somebody will say, "I hate to shop." Or, "I don't care about fashion." Or, "I don't have the money to look good." Or even, "I want people to like me for who I am inside, not for what I look like on the outside."

But those cop-out attitudes are definitely on the decline as people of all ages understand that looking good is a very large part of feeling good. And, as the fashion philosopher below wrote more than 40 years ago, it probably has always been.

> The extraordinary hold which the art (of fashion) has exercised upon its devotees is a measure of its historic importance. There has been no other of similar power with such continuous and widespread influence. It affects all classes and ages and has survived the forces of destruction which, temporarily, at least, have paralyzed other forms of artistic expression. It has held its own against even the assaults of religion, and in the many contests

waged between these opponents, the art of costume has never suffered a lasting defeat.... Despite them all, the wind of fashion bloweth..."
—C. Willet Cunningham in *Why Women Wear Clothes,* 1941

But many of us have never figured out the difference between *having style* and *being fashionable*—and it's this difference that counts.

Clara Hancox, noted men's wear commentator, put it this way when I asked her to discuss style and fashion.

"Style is *not* the same as fashion," she emphatically stated. "Style is the art of being the best you are—the creation of your own look, which comes from knowing yourself and finding what is out there to bring out the person you are.

"When people say, 'I like your style,' they're really saying, 'I like the way you see yourself.'

"Very often, *fashion* has no *style* at all. For instance, the mini-skirt may be fashionable at different times, but it is never truly stylish, no matter how many people wear it, or who designs its."

When a highly regarded mainstream designer such as Perry Ellis hangs his creative hat on a mini-skirt, a design last popular more than a decade ago, what should we think? Should those below-the-knee skirts in the closet be automatically reduced in size? Or should we try to understand why and how a designer decides to resurrect a fashion number *before* we do anything rash to our existing wardrobe or ravage our bank account in pursuit of the "new" fad?

"I asked Perry Ellis the same thing," said Clara Hancox. "And he told me: 'I get tired of looking at long, loose things, and I figure consumers must be tired too. So I'm shifting to short and tight.'"

The real change is that neither Perry Ellis nor most other top eighties designers expect that we will blindly follow their lead without thinking carefully beforehand.

Some people believe good looks can be bought, says Ellis. "People are enslaved to the cosmetics counter...designer clothes. Fashion designers can't make anybody look good. If you look good, my clothes support that in you. But looking good is feeling good, and feeling good is being at peace with yourself. If you're not sexy before you buy a dress, forget the dress."

"This is a very large country," adds Clara Hancox, "and *the word* today is, *wear it any way you please*—above or below, long or short, wide or thin. In a fashion-pervasive society like ours, the only thing *not* permitted is—ugliness."

Bill Blass put it well when he said: "You can look at it any way you want to, you can think about it, weigh it and get moralistic. But the truth is that looking good is the best revenge."

No, Bill, the truth is that looking good *in a bargain fashion* is the best revenge.

Groundrules for Bargain Chic

It's happened to all of us, no matter how much money we spend on clothes: Some days, without warning, the miserable moment strikes and you look in your closet and say, "I've got nothing to wear." No amount of mixing and matching will do. A nearby chair becomes a repository for rejected outfits. The only way out of the dressing doldrums, or so it seems as desperation overpowers the senses, is to buy something new. Or is it?

Going shopping at times such as these is like putting your finger in a hole in the dike. Even those of us who have been pursuing *bargain chic* for years must occasionally take stock of what we own—but rationally, at a time when the dressing doldrums have passed.

Stock taking. I do it seasonally, since I live in a part of the United States where I must have two fairly separate groups of clothing for different times of the year, as well as a growing

Looking good is the best revenge. Especially if you are wearing bargains like this season-spanning outfit. This pure silk blouse with cotton jersey collar and cuffs was reduced from $135.00 to $30.00. The matching pure cotton knit skirt was on sale at $13.00, reduced from $45.00 (Photo by Joan Tedeschi)

number of season spanners. In between the seasons, I occasionally flip through my acquisitions and arrange them according to type in order to reflect on my fashion future. Wherever you may be in your quest for style, it's important to *know what you have and where you are.* Be honest. I'll never part with some items of sentimental value, though I haven't worn them for years, and probably won't in the forseeable future. But what I don't feel sentimental or positive about, I periodically donate to charity, even if it's in good condition. Although it may pain you to throw hard-earned possessions out, it clears the mind—not to mention the closet—and paves the way for change.

Let's assume you've already got some standards in the closet—the bricks and mortar of your wardrobe. Whatever else you now buy must *fit in,* or at the very least, begin to take you in a viable new direction.

Unfortunately, when it comes to fashion bargains, some people become quickly demoralized after they make an impulse purchase of one of those on-the-cheap, one-of-a-kind, can't-wear-with-anything garments that, if only your *life* would change, you'd surely wear. People who begin bargain hunting in this way quickly conclude that sales are not for them.

So before you barge out on a bargain-hunting binge there are several steps you should take in order to get ready:

1. Take stock of the building blocks in your wardrobe that you can count on to support and tie into your new purchases—an item or two in each fashion category (shirts, trousers, skirts, sweaters, dresses, suits, jeans, shorts, etc.). Make lists, if necessary, to determine the apparel you care about, even if you haven't worn it recently. What about that favorite blouse you meant to find trousers for but never did? There will always be something you're not making good use of that can be recycled the *bargain chic* way.

2. Keep in mind whether these building blocks are prints or solids. Consider three or four color/print/fabric combinations you would like to create.

People used to think of fashion bargains as out-of-date and out-of-style. No longer. Fashion bargains are every bit as elegant and respectable as anything you'll find at full price. Some new bargain hunters will shout that from the roof tops. (Photo by Joan Tedeschi)

3. Even if you purchase a self-contained outfit on your bargain hunt, ask yourself whether it has multiple uses. If not, is it still worth buying?

4. All rules have exceptions, and here's a vitally important one to consider. If on your bargain travels, you discover an astoundingly valuable, incredibly cheap *something* that you know won't mesh with anything you already own, but (and this is the determinant) you really *will* wear, then *buy it*. Bargain hunting gives you the option of creating a sensible, stylish continuity in your clothing without spending too much; sometimes, when we meet up with an unusual bargain, it turns your best intentions upside down. That's okay, as long as the upside down bargains don't lead us permanently astray.

The same is true for the really good stuff that *isn't on sale*. Sometimes, maintaining a stringent *bargain chic* perspective can be painful—if you let it be. On an actual buying mission, stay positive by staying away from merchandise you can't afford. By now you know your stylistic preferences and how much you have to spend. It's fun to browse, but don't fritter away all of your time pining over those $150 cashmere sweaters that aren't reduced yet. Maybe next week. If you must try them, at the very least ask a salesperson if a sale on cashmeres is contemplated, and exactly when.

Countdown to Chic

We all dream at one time or another of being able to clear out our closets and start fresh. I've sometimes said to myself, "If somebody bequeathed me a few thousand dollars, why I could buy anything I wanted!" But reality intervenes. At any given time, even a budget of a few hundred dollars for clothes taxes my budget. The benefits of *bargain chic* save the day. Recently, after recognizing I had absolutely no dresses in my possession, I hooked a $130 Giorgio Sant'Angelo wool coat-dress for $19. I needed it as much as I wanted it. And at times such as this, I realize that even if my clothing budget were virtually limitless, no full-price item could elicit such a sense of accomplishment. Counting down to chic means *evaluation* and *creativity.* Here's how it works:

5. Think *inventory.* Be aware of *what you already have.* Ask yourself:
• Do I like my clothes?
• What would I change about them?
Don't expect to construct a new wardrobe overnight. Because if you do it that way, you might soon regret your impulsiveness. You've simply got to start somewhere, of course, but perhaps with one item that reflects who you are and how you want to be seen right now, and one or two others you can begin stocking for the season coming up.

4. Think *interchangeability.* Mix and match is an old phrase, but as timely now as ever. Begin by matching garments in your existing wardrobe to your new purchases. That way, you'll have twice as many outfits to choose from.

3. Think *season spanners.* Versatile fabrics, such as heavy cotton knits, fine wools, silks and some synthetic/natural fiber combinations can be worn throughout the year. Make wearability an important feature in the clothes you buy.

2. Think *color coordination.* Unless you're a genius at matching clothes culled from several disparate sources, you'll want to limit the color schemes in your closet. Dark or neutral colors are excellent building blocks. You can add flavor by using brightly hued accessories. If you have to purchase a completely unified "total look" every time you buy an outfit, you'll be spending far more than necessary.

1. Think *innovation.* If you own it already, don't buy it again. Take a chance on unusual fabrics and fashions, stores and styles. Reinvent yourself a little bit every day.

When you do, you'll be ready for induction into the army of guerrilla fighters in quest of the perfect bargain and the perfect wardrobe. Join us.

CHAPTER 2

Guerrilla Tactics for the Fashion Bargain Hunter

"The hunt, the search. That's the best part of bargains. The thrill is in the discovery, even more than the wearing. The thrill doesn't last forever, though I wish it would. But when you find something so terrific that it does give you that thrill, you feel chosen: This bargain had your name written on it. There's a cosmic intensity about it."

—Joan S., Museum Director

You might assume that with the profusion of sale merchandise, it would take no more than a casual stroll through a store to find the good stuff. And you could be right. But for more than beginner's luck, you will have to know where and when to look, and how to operate once you're in "enemy" territory, to tell the difference between a fair bargain and a sensational one. The more you save, the prettier the purchases look. So put on your battle fatigues—or whatever clothing you feel most comfortable wearing in the trenches—and let's begin basic training.

Locating the Store

It sounds easy to do, but the discerning bargain hunter always has his or her eyes and ears open to new stores and great buys. That means *research*. Haven't *time* for it? No library card needed. Just a few moments of your attention while reading the local daily and Sunday papers. Most major department stores advertise regular in-store and warehouse sales lavishly. Keep track of the *types* of sales that stores in your area offer, and how often they occur. When out for a drive on a lazy weekend afternoon, explore areas of your city. Shopping doesn't have to be your main objective. Keep a lookout for sale signs, especially in windows of smaller stores that may not advertise elsewhere. Scout a store inside, if you have time, making mental notes about what it offers, and don't be afraid to ask a salesperson the times when they customarily reduce their stock.

But you'll quickly discover that the best bargain research is by word-of-mouth.

- Do you have a friend or acquaintance whose fashion style you admire? Where do his or her clothes come from?
- At the office, barbecue or cocktail party, if you see the stylish person you've been quietly admiring blush when compliments are offered up, and you catch her saying, "Well, actually, I bought it on sale..." make friends with her quickly. She *knows* sales inside and out and is proud to say so.
- If you're a parent who frequents park benches or a neighborhood family center, keep your ears open for conversation about kiddie clothes. It often leads to suggestions about where to shop inexpensively.
- Consult directories of best buys, especially those which carry specific information about price, quality of merchandise and store location. Check local bookstores for regional directories (which are often printed privately) as well as magazine and newspaper columns dedicated to sales and bargain news. Here are a few national and well-known regional books to help you get started on the trail of *bargain chic*.

Bargain Finder: The Encyclopedic Money Saving Guide to New York City, by Eric Zuess, distributed by Golden Lee Books, Brooklyn, N.Y., $4.95.

Glad Rags II—A Directory to Discount Fashions in Los Angeles and Orange Counties, by Annette Swanberg and Leigh Charlton, Chronicle Books, $8.95.

SOS Save on Shopping Directory, by Iris Ellis, Villard Books, $10.95.

The 2nd Underground Shopper by Sue Goldstein, Andrews, McMeel, $7.95.

- When you see those newspaper ads for massive store sales, it might be a good idea to look over the merchandise if you have time. But don't actually *buy,* unless the bargain is too good to be true. Playing the waiting game is more fruitful. In the "In-Store Tactics" section, we'll tell you why. The *real* steals are usually available at the *very end of the sale,* or even after it's formally over. You may have to look more carefully for what you want, if the merchandise has been moved to a corner or a special "Clearance" area. These post-advertised sales are a bargain-lover's banana split.

In-Store Tactics

Immediately survey the area for signs. Some hang from ceilings, others from racks or are free-standing. Many stores print sales advisories to alert you to what is going on that day. Other places use public address systems to bring your attention to specials.

On your way to the department you want, take a look around, especially if the store is new to you. If it is a multi-level establishment, familiarize yourself with the layout. You may find what you're looking for on more than one level. I often just walk the length and breadth of each fashion floor to get a general feeling for the place. I initially keep my eyes

Never mind the full-price apparel. Make a beeline for any sign that offers you discounts on clothing classics you can put away for next summer, or winter. (Photo by Ebet Roberts)

focused slightly *above* the racks, where "Sale" signs should be, rather than on the clothes themselves.

Most every department in a department store offers *something* at a reduced price. The store's view is that a sale rack will whet your appetite for more costly items. But why give in? See if you can't find what you need amidst the bargains.

Smaller stores, too, usually have "sale" racks in the back. Before you purchase anything at full price, make sure something similar at one-quarter the price isn't tucked away on a rack with an obscured sale sign in the back corner next to some hissing water pipes.

Though fashions do change season to season, many basics stay the same, while others are altered imperceptibly. But since stores inevitably order anew, they must sell the old as fast as possible. Keeping this fact in mind is important at twice-yearly summer and winter season-end sales, or six to nine months later at the very *beginning* of the new summer or winter selling season, when leftovers are trotted out from storage and sold for a song. Trousers for $5 reduced from $50? Summer cotton jerseys plummeting from $24 to $4? Linen jackets just like the $70 new ones in the window, only you get them for $20 because they had their day in a cruise display a couple of months before. You can find bargains such as these!

Don't be afraid to explore the "As Is" rack, where a designer jacket lacking buttons or belt might be drastically reduced. In the old days, a store employed a seamstress to repair it. Today, it's more economical for the retailer to offer it at bargain rates to customers. Some imperfections are not noticeable except under a microscope, and can be obscured by an overblouse or belt; others can be mended effortlessly with needle and thread. On occasion I've come across a lovely item with terrible buttons. A side trip to a button store and you can make that bargain live.

When you find a fashion bargain and your usual size doesn't fit, try a size larger or smaller. It's common for top designers to cut their garments generously. That way, the consumer, fitting into a size smaller than usual, feels sleeker and more likely to buy. Sometimes, though, European-made garments in your usual size are on the snug side. If the quality of the garment and price are exceptional, set your ego aside. Besides, you can always cut out the size tag and no one but you will be the wiser.

If you see something "way out," maybe a green leather suede mini-skirt like the one my bargain-hunting friend Amelia describes in the "How They Do It" chapter, try it on. If it makes you feel good consider buying it even if your legs aren't your best feature. Many new fashions are meant to surprise and challenge our pre-conceived notions about how we look. This year's fad may be next year's standard. If the price is right, take a chance.

Often the good stuff is hidden in the back of the rack. Bargain mavens are natural burrowers. (Photo by Ebet Roberts)

Don't be afraid to utilize a store's "hold" or "layaway" policy. With a small downpayment (even if you don't have a charge account in a particular store), you may be able to reserve apparel you wish to purchase but can't afford to pay for in full right now. Pay in stages, and the item is yours. A store's "hold" policy may allow you to ponder the worth of a particular bargain you're just not sure about. They'll keep the item behind the counter while you go home and sleep on it.

Ask a salesperson if the store has a "Clearance Center," which may be located in a separate, cordoned-off area, or at a different address. Slogging through these areas can be hard work. Clothes are falling off hangers—half of them are on the floor or piled atop circular racks—and you can't count on any sort of organization by size. You'll have to pay your bargain dues by reading those tags that haven't been discarded, trying on anything that looks interesting, and making sure you'll have time to stand in the inevitable long lines at the dressing rooms and cash registers. Also, make sure *before* you begin that the "Clearance Center" takes checks or credit cards and that you are armed with the proper identification. There's nothing worse than finding one of those ultimate bargains and discovering you don't have the requisite cash to pay for it.

And don't forget, use your brain as a shopping resource. The price, quality and fashion information you collect over the years, coupled with your own highly cultivated instinct, is your best insurance against bargain mistakes—like the name-brand combination telephone-clock-radio I impulsively bought from a street vendor for $20. It was sealed in plastic, but... the radio has yet to play, and the phone periodically buzzes and refuses to process calls.

It's sometimes hard to keep a level head when you see that giveaway price—but if you don't, you'll be getting rid of your "prize" very soon.

I love this comment by Los Angeles bargain maven Viki King because it epitomizes the adventurous attitude of our breed: "People go into a store, They see something on a hanger. They say, 'That's cute.' Or, it's not cute and they don't even try it on. They only see it *on the hanger.* But they miss the point—they're the hanger! Clothing doesn't stand alone. It lives on a person. The person makes the difference."

How to Handle Salespeople

Have you ever noticed how differently you feel about stores? In some, you get the strong desire to buy everything. The milieu is perfect. In others, a chilly wind blows, pushing you out empty-handed. It's not only the decor, because stores that have virtually none at all may still exude warmth and personality. Indeed, how you feel about a store has as much to do with the people who run it as with the merchandise and ambience.

Though they exist to assist, salespeople often stand between you and your purchase. As a teenager I worked in the children's clothing department in a J. M. Fields' discount department store. Store morale wasn't very high: There was no telling when a person would be fired. My major task of folding kids' underwear didn't cheer me up, either. It was all I could do for the public to paste a wan smile on my face—until, sometime in a steamy July, I got my walking papers.

Not everybody has this perspective on the job of selling. Recalling my experience, I generally try to be cordial and patient with salespeople, but it's not always possible. Many of them are sullen and feel put upon. Bargain hunters bother them. Sometimes, when I ask one to check a price of an unmarked item on a sale rack, I get looks that could kill, or the whiny excuse that only the manager can help me and—you guessed it—the manager's out to lunch. Most lower echelon sales people work on hourly salary, and unless they've risen through managerial ranks or else accrued seniority, they're probably not very well paid. When we bargain mavens ask for special favors, their impulse is to ward off extra work.

Some salespeople, usually those stationed in men's suit departments, work on commission, which means they receive bonuses based on the dollar amount of sales they generate. Of course, these people tend to be more attentive and *very* persuasive if you are an indecisive shopper. One apparel chain executive I talked to boasted that because his employees did not work on commission they were never motivated toward the hard sell, but merely to assist pleasantly, when needed. However they're remunerated, salespeople have been hired to help, not to confuse and agitate you. One of the big issues facing today's traditional department stores is how to motivate employees and reinstitute the quality of service which once existed. It's within the rights of the consumer to demand the best "help." If you're not getting it, ask, complain, demand. When you find a truly helpful salesperson, thank your lucky stars, and the person, too.

Here's my breakdown of four common sales types, how to spot them and contend with them:

Type A—Aggressive: They unabashedly force themselves on you, even as you claim to be "just looking." You feel devious under their scrutiny, as if you'd better buy something quickly, without asking too many questions. They may not own the store, but they appear officious. You don't know quite how to act when they offer up a belittling remark about your fashion sense, hair style or shopping prowess, or begin invoking the names of famous designers and "the latest" styles.
SOLUTION: Ignore Type A and get on with the business of shopping.

Type B—Fawning: They rush to tell you everything looks great, even when you know it doesn't. Type A pushiness is evident in Type B, but in more palatable and subtle form. Theatrical Type Bs are capable of conning you into regrettable purchases. If you notice a salesperson wearing loose sleeves, you can be pretty sure he or she's a Type B. They laugh up that sleeve after you're gone.
SOLUTION: Know yourself. If it looks terrible to you, you'll hate it even more when you take it home.

Type C—Disinterested: Whatever you choose, however long you browse, Type Cs act as if you're invisible. They're usually extremely preoccupied with paper work or a telephone call from a friend, and couldn't care less about your needs, even when you stand directly in front of them, a patient look on your face, a question on the tip of your tongue. Try asking it and Type Cs will tell you to shush: "Can't you see how busy I am?" they hiss self importantly through the pursed lips.
SOLUTION: When Type Cs condescend to respond to consumer questions, they usually don't have the answer anyway. Seek out the manager or another, more willing salesperson.

Type D—Easy Going: The dream salesperson, who honestly wants to help, and offers advice only when you ask for it. Type Ds size you up accurately, and never attempt to inflict their own style sense. They're pleasant and cooperative, even after your kids terrorize the premises and you try on everything in the store and decide not to buy anything.

SOLUTION: Always ask the name of a Type D, easy going salesperson, and when you've made her a friend, attempt to learn as much as possible about the store's general sales policies.

Let Your Conscience Be Your Guide

Speaking of not buying anything, sometimes you feel the urge to shop, but haven't got the requisite funds. The determined bargain hunter uses such intervals wisely, in the service of education, by storing up information that will be useful when there is money to spend. But the bargain maven also exhibits admirable restraint, because no bargain is worth the ignominy of being unable to pay the bills. Back at the turn of the century, in her book *Secrets of Distinctive Dress*, Mary B. Picken addressed this very issue when she instructed readers to "make an exploit through your clothes closet. Then, when you have made a careful inventory, see whether your *conscience* will permit you to buy new clothes or not."

While you're not buying but are doing important research, it's necessary to give yourself an occasional bargain treat. Put aside $5 or $10 for those moments when you simply must exhibit *bargain chic.* You'll be amazed how satisfying a mini-binge can be.

And to save you from any other expenditures, here are four "Bargain Shopping Strategies When You Don't Have a Cent":

READ—I usually find fashion magazines thrilling and intimidating at the same time. I'm thrilled to be living in an age where fashion can be so inspiring and dynamic; intimidated by the underlying threat conveyed by fashion advertisements— "If you don't own this soon..." The ominous feeling passes, however, as soon as I turn the page. Fashion mags are meant to get the imagination cooking. The pictures we see are intended to create a sensation; they're usually considerably more outlandish than anything we'll ever see in the stores. Along with the photos are fashion stories. I prefer interviews that let designers talk about their own views. Compare them with your own expectations. If you can pick up one good tip per issue, and understand the intimidation factor for what it is, you're on your way, and I'll try to be on mine, too.

WALK—People who don't take shopping seriously can't figure out why it takes so much time. But it does and it should. When you're not buying, browse, window shop, try on, preferably when the season is still young and the stores full of the most up-to-the-minute fashions. Then you can go back later on to prowl among those same clothes for the bargains.

LOOK—At everybody else. I live near a public promenade and have spent many a Sunday afternoon watching the human parade. My husband criticizes jogging styles; I stick to fashion. And what an array! Sometimes, though, you can learn more from following the day-to-day dress-up spectacle of one person. A few years ago, I worked with a woman who really shook me to the foundations of my own style sense and possiblities. She was wealthy, and money was no object in her search for style. But she also *knew how to put it all together* in such a way that seeing her experiment with those aspects of fashion which delighted her—color, mixing fads with standards, accessorizing—was a real learning experience. When she entered a room, all eyes turned, and it wasn't because of her beauty; it was because of her style.

WATCH—If you live in a large city, check for department store or boutique sponsorship of occasional designer trunk fashion shows. What you see may be too expensive for your budget, but you'll have a head start in your search for substitutes. Many department stores are now also featuring video presentations of particular designer offerings—sometimes the actual Paris runway shows.

Have More Fun Shopping

Membership in a family means occasional forays shopping-as-a-family. Most of us are so familiar with the idiosyncracies of loved ones that we're able to cope with them even in an emotionally demanding shopping environment. But shopping with friends is an even more treacherous pursuit. A friend of mine was recently describing a shopping trip with another friend who had just expanded from 125 to 150 pounds but was convinced she was still a size 10. Their entire excursion was spent trying to wedge the woman into clothing much too small for her new personal dimensions. Yet there are fun ways to shop in groups, too, where the spirit of *bargain chic* lives. Here are some of them:

A Shopping Party: You used to do it as a teenager, making those shopping get-togethers with friends, sunrise to sunup with time out for tuna sandwiches or chow mein. Bring it up to date. Organize a Bargain Bash, with a fashion show at somebody's house to wrap things up. Who bought the most— and the best—for less? Award prizes. Swap bargain stories.

Second-Hand Sunday: Buy a map of your area. Check the "Garage," "Yard" and/or "Apartment Sales" section of your local newspaper. Map out the day's itinerary, and pick up new friends along the way. You'd be surprised how rummaging and ferreting out bargains in unlikely places can have, as a bonus, great conversation potential as you mingle with other hungry bargain bingers. Budget $10 or $20. You won't believe what you'll find...new...and used, starting at five and ten cents. Take time out for a picnic lunch.

Fashion Bargain Bus Party: With the advent of outlet malls and other super-duper shopping centers, you can economically charter a bus or van and discover stores outside your usual shopping radius. In outlying areas, hotels can be one of your best bargains, so stay overnight and make a weekend of it with your best bargain-hunting buddies.

Special Needs Shopping Extravaganza: Elderly or handicapped shoppers can make special arrangements with store managements to shop after hours. This is beneficial, especially during holiday times, when the store is so busy during regular business hours that it's hard for some people to shop effectively. Anybody who does this will have all the bargains to himself, and all the sales help he needs.

Invite a Pro: The burgeoning bargain trade has spawned experts available to lecture to your community or religious group about where, when, and how to shop. Phone the nearest mall or outlet center retailers' association for suggestions they may have about whom to approach. Some department stores also offer personal shopping services, and you might be able to engage a shopping expert from their ranks.

When to Say No to a Bargain

The more practiced you become at bargain hunting, the easier it will be to find ways to spend money. You may "save a fortune" every time out, but end up spending more money than you bargained for.

There was a time when I simply couldn't resist anything that was a bargain and looked good on me at the same time. But after a while I realized that many items that looked good didn't necessarily reflect my personality. I would wear them *because* they were bargains, not because I liked them. As I matured and discovered my own sense of style, I've been better able to ask the important questions *before* I bought a bargain, not after. The bottom line is that a truly good buy will be something you actually wear, not just stare at and continually push to the back of the closet.

What are the most effective ways to weigh your bargain investment? Here are my suggestions for sizing up the *particular* virtues and liabilities of your possible purchase.

Cost: Is it a bargain or isn't it? Markdowns come in all sizes. I enjoy the $10 to 99 cent variety, and won't think twice about handing over a dollar for a fun accessory that costs less than a tuna fish sandwich at a diner. But as our taste becomes more sophisticated, so may the bargains that catch our eye, like the designer coat marked down to $100 from $300. Don't be blinded by a reduction of two-thirds, or seduced by the famous label. Before you snap it up, think: if the same coat were originally priced at $100, would you have given it a thought? No? Then put the coat back.

Quality: Not all apparel is meant to last forever, fashion- or quality-wise. I bought my first ultra-wide, low-slung belt for $4 from a street corner vendor for a reason: I just didn't know if the style was right for me. In that sense, the belt was a bargain; for very little, it helped me experiment and learn. It didn't matter to me when it fell apart after a dozen wearings. My next belt was a more expensive bargain.

Quality is a vitally important aspect of a bargain when the garment or accessory is earmarked to be a wardrobe standard, or, at the very least, a standard for a season. You want it to survive. So as you weigh the virtues, say, of a bargain rate 100 percent acrylic sweater and one with wool content that may prolong its life and its looks, make an educated guess about the value of each, not just in dollar terms. How long you expect to have a garment and how many times you expect to wear it have a lot to do with whether it's a bargain or a burden purchase.

Maintenance: Clothes need care, some more than others. My mother's view about blouses has always been that "If you can't throw it in the wash, then it's not a bargain." It's true that if you purchase a silk blouse at a discount, you're going to have to "pay" in time terms if you wash and iron it yourself, and in fairly steep and regular economic terms if you choose to have it pressed professionally. But if that blouse will be pivotal to the success of several outfits, it can still be as good a buy as the price tag indicates.

Bargains Now, Bills Later

My bargain hunts have always been aided and abetted by charge cards. On the days when my bargain radar is really working, I never seem to be carrying cash. When that bargain rears its beautiful head, out comes the little plastic card. Of course, it's easy to rationalize that if I don't buy now, I'll end up paying much more later on.

Does having charge cards at the ready mean I spend more for bargains? Maybe sometimes. (If you worry about this, maintain a very low dollar maximum with your cards. It will prevent you from careless usage.) For me, a card provides just a convenient way of deferring costs, especially if I hadn't originally planned to buy clothes that week. With two or three charge cards, you can judiciously stagger your clothing expenses, according to each card's monthly billing date. Also, be quite sure that the cards to which you subscribe don't unduly penalize you for occasional non-payment—and, most important of all, that you don't become a charge card junkie. No fashion bargain is worth that price.

When a Bargain Costs Full Price

Don't let your bargain mentality prevent you from enjoying occasional full-price flings, especially if the garment will prove pivotal to your wardrobe. I bought two items of apparel last winter that weren't exactly on sale, though each was an example of good value. I picked up the top I'm wearing in the photo on the back cover of this book in Montreal, a fashion capital where, just as in many other countries, U.S. citizens can make use of the advantageous exchange rate to save money. I paid $48 for this cotton-wool-leather combination garment, which I felt would have cost twice as much in the States. And I recently bought an elegant wool and leather skirt for more than I've ever paid for a skirt—$80. Why? Because the wool knit was fine, the leather supple, and the skirt was cut exactly right for me. It was originally part of a two-piece outfit; since someone had pilfered the top, the boutique owner sold me the bottom half at a discount.

These two items have proven to be signposts for my current wardrobe. The top won't be wearable forever—it's too trendy. But I've worn it time and again, and it fits in everywhere. The skirt will, I hope, go on forever. And I love and appreciate each of these purchases, for what they do for my psyche and my body! Here are my suggestions for times when you should stress the *chic* in *bargain chic:*

1. When you've never seen anything so terrific in your life.
2. When you're going to wear it all the time, with all the other superb markdowns in your closet.
3. When you have no time to find a bargain.
4. When it's a gift.

CHAPTER 3

What Kind of Shopper Are You, Anyway?

A BARGAIN SHOPPER'S AFTERSHOCKS

A Cautionary Tale in Three Acts

I. Euphoria!

You can't believe it. You've outwitted the designer, the manufacturer, the store. Everybody else must be blind, including other consumers. Clutching your purchase as you would a sack of gold, you feel like "Shopper of the Year." Arriving home, you feverishly rip open the bag, caress your discovery and immediately call friends and relatives to share the wealth or just gloat. If you live with someone else, you force him to listen to a blow-by-blow description of your shopping victory, exclaiming what a lucky break it was that it matches your new green shoes so perfectly. Then you quietly retire to another room to proceed with a very private fashion show in front of the mirror where nobody can see you.

All this giddiness leads to . . .

II. Regret.

Suddenly you cannot believe how fat (or skinny) you look, how pale (or florid). The seat of your bargain pants is ripped—and you didn't even notice. Even if you sew it up, which would only take a few minutes, there's a dismaying fade mark on the crease and the color somehow looked less garish under the store's fluorescent lights. You take those new green shoes from the closet—the ones you should have brought with you—and find that the colors clash miserably. That means you'll have to shop again for that perfect match.

This predicament leads to...

III. Embarassment.

This mistake is so *bad,* so dreadful in its implications that the thought of returning it to the store is more than you can bear. And where's the sales slip? You were in such a hurry to get home that you left it on the counter, or maybe you threw it out with the wrapper from the candy bar you demolished in order to replenish your energy after the big bargain purchase. Your roommate waits with something less than bated breath to see the "Bargain of the Year" modeled in all its glory. Now the real "schlock aftershock" hits, the awful realization that you whipped yourself into such a bargain frenzy that you literally lost your mind and ended up with—in a word—junk. Take cover. But having experienced the depths of bargain bingeing, you can now go on to scale its peaks!

Your Shopping Personality

Bargains are great fun to find and an enormous asset to any wardrobe built on a shoestring. But the rewards are in direct proportion to the skill employed in their discovery and how successfully you integrate them into an existing wardrobe.

Information about where to find bargains, clothing and otherwise, isn't very helpful if your basic beliefs and perspectives on sale goods—and on shopping in general—are skewed. Consumers today must be brighter than ever. In the old days, you bought the calico the only shopkeeper in town stocked. You trusted the shopkeeper and the quality of the material.

Today, the choices about what to buy, where to shop and how much to spend are positively endless, and often exceedingly confusing. How to be stylish? How to feel good about shopping? And how to have money left over afterward? These are questions most of us ask, and we're so desperate for answers that we buy millions of magazines every month to help us.

But the basic questions remain largely unanswered because of our helter-skelter consumer approaches to the marketplace. One or more of the shopping flaws exhibited in this shopper's survey may prevent you from the pleasure of knowing how and when to buy bargains.

Here's my circus gallery of common shopping types. *Which kind of shopper are you?*

The Picayune Shopper will always browse the sale racks hoping for a bargain that will be a suitable substitute for a full-price item. But compromise for the sake of saving money? No way. Picayune finds the satisfaction of a bargain secondary to the pleasure of purchasing a perfect specimen. Usually, in Picayune's view, sale merchandise is either too long or too short, too plain or too busy, too cheap or too fine. Virtually nothing can satisfy Picayune, who owns very few clothes in very few styles, and probably doesn't even like them very much.

TIP—It's okay to take some personal and fashion risks. Nobody will hold it against you if what you decide on doesn't last forever. Consider that because you're bored you may not like the clothes you already own or are buying. A bargain may be just the thing; it won't cost you much to experiment to find a "new you."

The Tornado Shopper blitzes through stores like an Olympic runner. Tornado is an experienced bargain shopper who avoids a sign that says "New For Spring," knowing it usually coincides with a companion rack offering 50 percent off on *current* fashions. Once Tornado locates the clearance racks, bargain osmosis begins. In a flash, Tornado searches for tiny visual clues to a garment's quality, price and value, gently brushing the corner of a sleeve or the inside of a collar or waistband to get a "psychic feel" for the bargain potential of the merchandise. Occasionally, on a hunch, the Tornado pushes the rack to one side to survey a particular find more carefully. Tornado isn't afraid of nooks and crannies, apparel jammed into corners, soiled or fallen beneath the rack to the floor. In a flash, aided by built-in bargain radar, Tornado blazes to another department for an even better bargain.

TIP—The Tornado Shopper possesses self-assurance and speed on the job, encyclopedic wardrobe knowledge and an eye for fashions of the moment. But so quick to judge is this bargain maven, that sometimes the best buys are overlooked. If you are a Tornado, slow down. Many stores are open seven days a week. You needn't scurry around like a chicken with his head cut off. Your attitude toward bargain buying is great, but economy shopping doesn't mean moving at a breakneck pace which may hinder your ability to make wise choices.

The Assignment Shopper shops with only specific items in mind: A pair of blue shoes to match a certain blue-ish sweater that seems to be the *only* thing appropriate to wear on Saturday night to a particular dinner party. The Assignment Shopper's stop-gap mentality precludes most bargains. If a pair of black shoes are on sale that day, the Assignment Shopper won't give them a thought—until next week, when Assignment suddenly realizes it's black, not blue, on which the wardrobe hinges. Then, it's out again to comb the stores. Mission: black, even when the bank account is definitely...blue.

TIP—Don't always be so particular. If you're more flexible, you'll find bargains in the most unlikely places and at the most unlikely times. Open yourself up to some of them...take chances. And get to know a Tornado Shopper.

The Deadline Shopper: Waiting 'til the last minute, this breed rushes into a store with special needs but is limited by time and place. Money is usually of secondary concern to Deadline, who has enough trouble finding the right merchandise at full price. Under the gun, Deadline feels so anxious and pressured to perform correctly that rash, regrettable decisions often ensue.

New bargain hunters never pass up the opportunity to burrow in piles of unfolded, unheralded goods. Often, the best buys are hidden at the bottom. (Photo by Joan Tedeschi)

Tɪᴘ—Try to plan ahead in terms of your schedule and budget. You'll have more options—and savings to the pocketbook—if you do.

The Buddy System Shopper can't seem to make any fashion purchases without someone to point out the virtues of the apparel. Buddy Shoppers—and men proliferate in this category—are particularly wary of signs or advertisements promising apparel at bargain rates. Buddy *wants* to buy, but it's always up to the friend to flatter him into making a decision—any decision. Buddy, however, is easily burned by leaning too heavily on another's judgment. At home, the bargain pales, and poor Buddy is even more wary the next time he goes shopping, especially if what he just bought and dislikes was a bargain.

Tɪᴘ—Just once, try being your *own* fashion consultant. You may make mistakes, but you'll develop a flair for what's really "you." And don't be so frightened of that four-letter word—ꜱᴀʟᴇ —that you've been avoiding. You'll really feel powerful if you find something just right—and at half off, too!

The Compulsive Shopper is so skilled at discovering bargains that for him to leave a good deal on the rack is a fate worse than death. Instead, Compulsive will buy multiples of every bargain and will rationalize these extra purchases by promising to give them as presents to friends and family. Compulsive ends up spending so much money on extras that the savings disappear. Even when Compulsive cleans out the store, satisfaction is fleeting. Very likely, Compulsive's unquenchable appetite for shopping will draw him to make more impulsive purchases. By the time Compulsive arrives home, the compelling need surfaces to shop again. Compulsive may periodically be forced to hold an apartment or garage sale to make room for new tonnage.

Tɪᴘ—A "bargain" is only a bargain if you can use it now or in the very near future. Your friends and family can shop for themselves. You can even call them from the store if you see something too good to pass up. Remember, the store will be there tomorrow with new—perhaps better—bargains. Take a chance by *not* buying today.

The Fad Shopper buys everything in "fashion," even if it looks tacky. Fad willingly takes fashion risks, is not afraid to offend, and usually does. Since "fad" clothes are often inexpensively mass produced, when the next fad emerges, Fad's existing wardrobe is in tatters, and good old Fad is ready to jump on board the next bandwagon.

Tip—Start living for tomorrow as well as today, by building a wardrobe that makes use of classics as well as forgettables.

The After-I-Finish-the-Diet Shopper always buys everything one size smaller than necessary. By the time it fits—if ever—it's inevitably out of style. After-I-Finish-the-Diet inevitably sports poor coloring because the clothing is so tight. The clothes she has chosen are not slimming—in fact, they're quite the opposite. This shopper is so depressed about this state of affairs that the diet is put off until next season.

Tip—Face it. You deserve to look nice now, and can buy clothes today—on sale—that will help you look and feel thinner, even if you're not.

The High Living Shopper, partial to fashion-forward clothing, is inevitably attracted to expensive designer labels priced far beyond her means. High Living has good taste and knows and demands quality. Viewing sale merchandise as suspect, High Living would never be caught dead even looking at the 75-percent-off rack.

Tip—Take that peek at the 75-percent-off rack. We won't tell. And you *will* find quality and fashion because *you* know what you're looking for!

The "That's Nice But Not for Me" Shopper has a built-in negativity monitor. When new fashion trends appear, this individual instantly regrets personal height, weight, coloring, facial features, neck size, arm length, leg shape and behind. On a shopping trip, "That's Nice But Not for Me" veers toward clothing that is shapeless, colorless and uninteresting, and wistfully compliments friends on their more daring wardrobes.

Tip—This "imperfectly" built shopper is correct in questioning the appropriateness of some styles, but is being unfairly deprived of looking and feeling more "with it" by an outdated, even prim, sensibility. In an "anything goes" society, you can take chances like never before.

The Cheapskate Shopper loves bargains, but hardly ever buys them, or anything at all, for that matter. Cheapskate always figures tomorrow the sales will be even better. Cheapskate's "wait and see" policy masks a terrible case of indecision that inevitably bars Cheapskate from the enjoyment of looking good. So on those rare occasions when Cheapskate does make a purchase, it's inevitably passé, slightly too big or too small, with imperfections and bizarre elements that make it virtually unwearable.

Tip—The bigger the reduction, the better the buy? Not necessarily so, Cheapskate. Allow yourself the pleasure of a medium-range bargain, say 50 percent off the original price for starters. Feed your need for rock-bottom buys on little accessories while building up your wardrobe with apparel that is as pretty to look at as it is prettily priced.

The Ideal Shopper has taken the time to assess color preferences, cultivate a sense of style, an understanding of quality, and a keen belief in value. Ideal's lifestyle is well served by this wardrobe collected on a shoe string which carries on nobly through permutations of fashion fancy. Ideal experiments, but is self-aware enough to bypass fads that do not fit. Budget-minded without being penny-pinching, Ideal weighs the benefits of sale merchandise against that at full price and is not blinded by designer labels. An organized person with a sense of humor about clothing, Ideal plans ahead, rarely buys at the last minute, and almost always looks elegant. Ideal is willing to risk a few bargain binge mistakes a year, but never loses that sense of adventure and awe brought about by bargain beauties. Ideal has class and confidence, and even when appearing to make a wrongheaded fashion decision, can still pull it off with—here's that word again—style!

CHAPTER 4

Department Stores

Few of them remain—those overheated, downtown caverns of
clothing with the grayish walls of a penal institution, wheezing
cash registers, dim lighting and the heat turned up to 90
degrees. The gnarled salesladies were programmed to say,
"May I help you, dearie?" They adored everything you put on
and barged into the dressing room without knocking, just as
you had stripped down to your birthday suit. (Did these ladies
actually live somewhere else besides the store. Did anybody
ever love them? It was impossible to imagine. Was there a
retirement home in the sky for salesladies? When I wasn't
prowling for bargains I had these peculiar thoughts.)

To stave off the incursion of giant discounters, boutiques,
malls and off-pricers and to fight the decline of city centers,
department stores molted out of necessity and moved to the
suburbs. And while most bargain mavens probably cut their
shopping teeth in lumbering old flagship department stores,
their modernized counterparts haven't let us down. When
they embarked on a course of shopping history that made every
day a sale day, bargain mavens were blissfully happy.

In fact, the word sale has become synonymous with department store policy in all but the most ritzy establishments. It
happened almost overnight.

In the 1970s, accomplished at sitting on their laurels, department stores wrongly figured *their* customers wouldn't be
caught dead shopping those new fangled stores called off-pricers.
Loehmann's in New York and Filene's Basement in Boston had
been around for decades, but were no more than a small an-

noyance to department stores. When Loehmann's began its spread over the U.S., Syms along the Southeast corridor, Boltons in the New York metropolitan area and Ross Stores and C and R Clothiers grew on the West Coast, department stores remained surprisingly aloof.

Shopping off-price was "fine for some people, but not *our* customers," executives intoned in department store board rooms. And if women of means were known to frequent New York's Lower East Side on Sunday mornings for designer frocks at half price, that didn't stop them from showing up Monday to shop full-price.

Now department stores know better. They learned the hard way—by watching new, cut-rate retailers syphon off some 10 percent of their customers. Still, some department stores continued to protest that their clientele *was* different, that service and environment mattered. Meanwhile, round table discussions were held in the trade to discuss how to encourage loyalty and courtesy in sales staffers whose reputation for cordiality and knowledgeability had seriously eroded and the store's business with it.

While criticizing the rise of off-price, cut-rate retailing, and lobbying in Washington with some success to reinstitute manufacturers' minimum retail pricing to undermine its growth, the biggest names in department store ownership have created their own or bought into thriving off-price chain operations that have been spreading like wild fire in the past five years. Federated now owns Filene's and the Children's Outlet chains; U.S. Shoe created T. H. Mandy and Little Folks; Melville Corp. launched Marshalls; Woolworth founded J. Brannam; Zayre created T. J. Maxx and Hit or Miss; May Department Stores launched the Venture discount division; Associated Dry Goods recently bought Loehmann's. Even so, the very best department stores are continuing to evolve, to reflect the new needs of a changing work force ever more populated by women, and the demands of American men and women with growing leisure-time fashion needs. The biggest and best of these stores are also building—Bloomingdale's has now opened stores in Dallas and Miami, for instance.

With this expansion and re-direction, we sale mavens are raising important questions that department stores are busy trying to answer. Can they continue to serve us at the low, low prices we require? Are their sales worthwhile from the bargain shopper's perspective? Here are some additional questions every bargain hunter needs answered when shopping in department stores:

- How much money is really saved when a department store launches a full-page ad in your local paper, announcing 25 percent off almost everything in the store?
- Are goods offered by department stores superior to or the same as those of off-pricers and many discount department stores? And who actually gets them first?

Although surely there are exceptions, some department stores, in order to make a profit on those increasingly frequent sale days, have resorted to a clever—if spurious—pricing system. As a number of industry observers have described this process, the retail price of many goods are inflated at the outset. When the first 25-percent-off sale is announced, only then is the item priced where it should be. Department stores know that the four letter word s-a-l-e, however flimsy its promise, is enough to get consumer juices flowing. Yet undiscerning bargain shoppers who hop to the dance of a sale without thinking and comparing won't really save a cent.

It's true that many department stores are still sometimes "first" by a few weeks to display select fashion-forward merchandise. Special fall fashions purchased in small quantity may be on the floor of these establishments three or four months before anybody can wear them. Impulsive full-price fashion-forward shoppers who had to be the first on the block to wear Perry Ellis's new mini, for instance, willingly paid a premium to flaunt it.

Yet as off-pricers now order such huge quantities of clothing and pay for it much more quickly, manufacturers and designers are more willing than ever to sell to them even as they protest publicly that they never would. In fact, industry statistics now show that, more than half the time, leading off-pricers receive quality goods *as early in the season as department stores!* And unlike most department stores, "dis-kies," as they're sometimes called behind-the-scenes, demand no special compensations, such as cooperative advertising or "markdown money" that is paid if the apparel doesn't sell at full price and must be "reduced for quick sale."

So what *can* department stores offer fashion bargain hunters?

Selection. At full price, department store apparel may not be a bargain hunter's dream, but it soon can be. By virtue of their size, these establishments have enormous amounts of clothing constantly coming in—and they have to sell what they already have in stock. That means scheduled markdowns which, by the middle of the winter or the middle of the summer, are substantial—often 30 to 70 percent off the original price. There will often be a great selection of sale items, in *many* departments, usually grouped by brand or designer name, price and style.

Great Sale Flukes. Again because department stores are so huge, there are many different buyers marking down all the time. Sometimes, a nifty little item becomes a super bargain because the buyer wants to get rid of it. Storing merchandise is costly and, unlike an off-pricer whose clientele expects to find some outdated apparel, department stores can't sell it next season at a profit. Also, the sheer number of departments can be a boon. On your way to the coat area, for example, you pass the shoes and *voila!* There are the boots you need but hadn't planned to buy until next week. And at half price. I have found more rock-bottom fashion sale bargains, in the 75 to 90 percent category, in department stores than anywhere else. The flagship Abraham & Straus (A&S) near my home has always relegated junior sportswear specials to out-of-the-way corners on the 4th floor, and as a matter of course I check them out each time I'm in the store. Recently, they had suede jackets reduced from $79 to $19 tucked on the far side of a circular rack in the lower depths of the coat department. Literally *every* department in that store has such an unheralded area, and I've virtually clothed my entire family from them. When I go home to Rochester, New York, I'm amazed and delighted that McCurdy's, one of that city's venerable department stores, continues to place its reduced apparel on the same racks that I used to haunt 20 years ago as a high school student!

Aside from such clearance sales, there's usually at least one department store in a major city with a reputation for a once-or-twice-a-year, rock-bottom sale of the best goods, or else a special department or warehouse where terrific, timely designer-quality merchandise is dumped for the smart shopper's pleasure.

Pre-Holiday Specials. It used to be that all the sales *followed* the holidays. Now, as people tend to hold on to their money to the last minute rather than spend it, department stores are reducing items *in advance* of Christmas, July Fourth, Washington's Birthday, Mother's Day and every other real or imagined holiday we have to stimulate sales. Last year my children needed snow jackets, and as I was browsing in a Penney's store in August, I discovered some wonderful jackets *already* discounted by 30 percent off that store's very good prices. Sometimes the pre-holiday savings in department stores dip to as much as half the original price.

Here are just a few of these marvelous sale inventions and the stores and cities where they can be found. With very little investigating you can discover which stores in your area do the same.

Rich's (Atlanta). Their fifth floor sale is called "Final on 5," all year round.

Jordan Marsh (Boston). Bargain Basement along the lines of Filene's, also of Boston and Long Island, N.Y.

Sach's (Detroit). Christmastime, one-week-only American/ European designer clothes sale.

Alexander's (New York). Second floor bargain corner where women's fashions from all over the store are brought; First Floor bargain section.

Robinson's (Los Angeles). Flagship store clearance center.

Bonwit-Teller (New York). Seasonal sales culminating with appearance of racks of designer clothing set in the center of the aisles of the store.

Barney's (New York). This swanky mostly-men's fashion department store is known for it's occasional warehouse blow-out, always advertised in the newspapers and always heavily attended.

Abraham & Strauss (Brooklyn) Giant new basement-level fashion clearance center (Filene's, look out!).

Private Label Bargains. With the rise of designer-for-less retailers, department stores have resorted increasingly to manufacturing merchandise exclusively their own. And some of it is very good—highest quality workmanship and styles resembling noted fashion brands. Carter Hawley Hale offers no less than 14 private labels, including Cassis and Cadaz, to its member stores; Frederick Atkins, a central buying and research office for 40 major U.S. department stores, uses the Jonathan Stewart and Christian Aujard private labels in stores such as A, M and A (Buffalo); B. Altman (New York); The Broadway (L.A.); Dillards (Little Rock, Ft. Worth, San Antonio); Hess's (Allentown, Pa.) and John Wanamaker (Philadelphia). The Dayton-Hudson chain of stores now uses its own Boundary Waters line; the Associated Dry Goods chain of department stores stocks 18 private labels, including the Alan Solly line of men's wear at Abraham & Straus in the New York area; Macy's on both coasts now uses Great Plains for a line of in-house jeans, and Club-house for sportswear.

J.C. Penney's, in a real industry coup, now contracts new, value-priced, exclusive designer lines from Halston, Ann Klein and Lee Wright in its stores.

The original retail price of private label goods should be about 20-30 percent less than comparable designer brands, because a store is cutting out the middleman when it does its own manufacturing. Reductions of private label goods are often unadvertised—you'll have to scout the store to find them. But when private label goods are then reduced even 25 percent, you'll end up saving much more if the merchandise compares favorably to well-known, higher-priced brands.

One-Stop Bargain Shopping. For those who don't have time to scout the malls and shopping center boutiques, and/or simply get confused by roaming the endless mall or outlet center bargain range, department stores offer the benefit of apparel for the whole family under one roof and a variety of sales people to point you in the right direction. Department stores are almost never claustrophic, as many smaller boutiques can be. Since shopping is more anonymous, you don't leave feeling you've personally offended the sales help if you haven't found exactly what you need.

Fashion Spectrum Shopping. People of varying lifestyles can all find a home in the average department store, which cannot afford to forget either the executive, laborer, homemaker, teen, retiree or tot. Under one roof are the latest fads and the classics. Department stores are perfect for one-stop family shopping without losing somebody along the way.

And they continue to offer customers a range of service benefits:

- Flexible return and exchange policies.
- Telephone, catalog and mail order shopping.

- Convenient in-store restaurants, telephones and restrooms; photo studios; beauty shops.
- Gift wrapping (for a fee) and gift boxes (usually free with proof of purchase).
- Charge accounts and installment buying.
- Personalized shopping experts.
- In-store alterations.

But that's not enough for some stores. Newer innovations include updated and streamlined bridal and layette registeries run by computer (Macy's, Filene's, Dayton's); corporate gift services (Marshall Field); credit cards for minors (Buffums, California); apartment-finders (Woodward and Lathrop, Washington, D.C.); and auto leasing (Rich's, Atlanta).

Improving the quality of sales help is another large priority. The 11-store Batus chain, for example, has a new program, named CARE (Customers are Really Everything). Three years ago, the Gimbel's Midwest division of Batus began giving employees $5-a-day bonuses to up their personal selling records. On the first day sales nearly doubled.

Marshall-Field in Chicago began a "White Carnation" campaign in which its 1,000 executives and managers could be easily identified to customers requiring assistance, by flowers in their lapels.

Add to all these shopping values the feeling of intimacy and warmth you can develop for a department store, or how spectacularly decorative many of the best ones have now become. Shopping department stores is almost like going to the theater or art museum in some cities. Department stores such as I. Magnin, Nieman-Marcus, Bloomingdale's, Sakowitz and others in the first rank go all out on displays and store-wide theme ventures that provide shoppers with a look at style from foreign perspectives. Eventually, of course, some of the clothes imported for these festive occasions will be on sale! As long as you know how to find the bargains, what a nice plus that is.

Nobody knows how long department stores will be sale-tripping, whether the innovations currently in the works will resurrect their status and eliminate the need for sales. But as one industry observer put it: "Nobody takes the automobile sticker price too seriously anymore, and the exact same thing is happening to retailing." That just might mean that the bargains WILL continue in department stores, even as the service and the ambience continues to be enhanced. And that's good for *bargain chic*.

CHAPTER 5

Off-Price Stores

"Generally speaking, when people go to off-price
and factory outlet stores, we don't have to sell *to*
them. They come to buy."

—Monroe Milstein,
Burlington Coat Factory

Although the most venerable off-price chains and boutiques
have existed for decades—Loehmann's started in 1921 in an
ornate Brooklyn mansion where the comfy chairs served as
respite for the put-upon husbands of bargain shoppers—the
tiny, cramped designer fashion discount stores of New York
City's Lower East Side were *the* place for shoppers in the know.
Before that, they bought designer fashions for less from pushcart
vendors!

But it wasn't until the late 1970s that off-price made a
difference in the retail marketplace. It was the first new twist
in shopping since catalog showrooms struck the public's fancy
the decade before. And in practically no time, spurred by the
lagging economy of the early 1980s, off-price shopping
quickly came of age.

When I discovered the one off-pricer in Buffalo, N.Y.,
where I lived in the middle 1970s, it quickly became my
favorite payday haunt. Located just too far downtown to be
fancy, Syms pushed as much apparel onto its racks as
possible, and it was up to the customer to weed out the
goodies. The decor was forgettable, the bargains memorable,

that's precisely how Sy Syms and other early off-price stores wanted it. His advertising slogan said it all: "An educated consumer is our best customer."

I vividly remember my weekly snooping sessions, especially at the $5 rack where I once picked up an uncut silk skirt and matching tunic, and the time the sprinklers went off unannounced directly on one or two of the men's classy vyella wool shirts. All were immediately reduced from Syms's already low price of $28 to $3, along with the cottons, too. The thing that stuck in my feverish bargain hunter's mind after that smorgasboard (which enabled my graduate student husband to look more like a full professor) was how quickly off-pricers dealt with catastrophe by being even nicer to shoppers than usual. No newspaper come-ons announcing SPECIAL FIRE SALE—100 MEN'S SHIRTS, 45 TIES—just the goods marked for quick and painless disposal.

Meanwhile, department stores were thrashing about, offering the usual holiday sales, holding out as bastions of retail superiority. In most cities one or two traditional stores began operating on a semi-off-price system, where, alongside "suggested retail," were some very nice branded bargains.

In the four years between '79 and '83, off-pricers surprised their competition as they grew by 23 percent a year. By 1985, they represented about a 10 percent share of retail fashion, with projected growth to between 12 and 20 percent by 1990. "As long as we have a lower rate of growth of real income, discount stores and factory outlets will continue to thrive. The consumer wants more steak and less sizzle today," was how marketing expert Peter LaPlace, of the University of Connecticut, put it recently.

That's why, though department stores only recently began reckoning with this upstart breed, most of us had begun to do so a while back. The off-price explosion really meant that consumers would just have to do a little research to figure out who had the "real" bargains, and who didn't.

The best off-price establishments have made shopping an adventure and a bargain at the same time. Operating in most instances minus frills, which means fewer sales help, off-pricers discovered that independent-minded shoppers didn't care about personal service as much as they did about quality. In a 1984 study of the shopping habits of working women, more than 50 percent preferred shopping *without* sales help when buying clothes for themselves; when buying for their kids, they were even more adamant: 80 percent said they'd rather do it without assistance. The study, conducted by the Associated Merchandising Corporation, also found that:

- The average off-price shopper, 37 years old, with a household income of $40,000, considered value the most important factor in the purchase of apparel.
- 44 per cent *only* bought clothing on sale.
- 67 per cent were comparison shoppers.
- 51 per cent felt the inventories of off-price establishments were as contemporary as those of department stores.

Indeed, the image of the discounter as a purveyor of seconds and irregulars, last century's fads, odd lots and leftovers, imported clothing ripped by over-zealous customs agents, and the soggy remains of flash floods and fires, has been superseded.

The new off-price image is of stores pursuing the most highly sought-after designer name brands, and while it would not be possible to list all notable off-pricers, the competition includes Hit or Miss (more than 200 stores nationwide), J. Brannam's two-dozen locations, Donlevy's Back Room (more than 30 stores), some 70 Fashion Barn stores, and nearly 100 T. J. Maxxes. All of these are off-price chain store divisions of giant department store groups with built-in clout with manu-facturers and designers; independent "disky" chains include Burlington Coat Factory, which boasts some 70 stores in 29 states across the U.S., each with more than 60,000 square feet of room for bargains, bargains, bargains.

The tendency is to lump all off-pricers together, but it is misleading to do this without taking positioning into account. In some stores, the intention is to overwhelm you with merchandise, hoping a vast inventory will impress you—and stimulate you to buy—even when the goods lack distinction. Stock in some stores is a motley collection of "opportunity" purchases by the retailer, timely deals that may look better to him than to his customers. These "opportunities," or "specials," in O-P lingo, might include:

- LYs—last year's.
- Dogs—rejects.
- Overruns and oddlots (extras of every type from the factory).
- Total closeouts (there's no more where these came from).

Take your pick, and if you pick carefully, you *may* just unearth an incredible must-buy. As one off-pricer described such a store: "If you go into it, one week it's coats they're pushing, tons and tons of coats, at a very good price. But you'd better *need* a coat, otherwise you'll leave empty-handed. The next week, it's sweaters. Whatever they don't have, they couldn't get a good deal on, and the customer will have to wait."

Other off-pricers have style on their minds along with a variety of goods year round. As Karen Glance, Director of Operations of Boltons, a growing New York metropolitan area women's off-pricer, remarks: "The word 'discount' is so abused. Some stores are discounters but they don't have a real merchandise mix or philosophy, both of which are important at Boltons.

"Our priorities are style, color, fashion timelessness, balanced stock and assortment. Because we turn over goods so fast, we can also get them as quickly as anybody else. We go in to buy legitimately, like any other retailer, and we buy more so it costs us less and we pass less of a markup on to the customers. Unlike department stores," Glance continues, "if an item does well in early tests, we go back and keep stocking it through the season, while they will perhaps restock only once and then go on to the next season, months in advance, while most people are still wearing and buying for the current season. Yes, occasionally we will be weak for a short time in one area, *because* we are a discounter, but that happens less and less often these days."

While manufacturers and designers publicly protest that they'd *never* sell goods to odious off-price types, many now do so on the sly, or through middlemen called "jobbers" and "diverters." Protecting their channels of distribution can sometimes get hairy, but the off-pricers are working hard to ensure us our bargains. In 1983, the Kids 'R' Us off-price clothing division of Toys 'R' Us, sued General Mills's Izod division, as well as Absorba, when these entities, under pressure from a huge department store conglomerate, refused to sell to them. Soon after, Burlington Coat Factory Warehouse charged the same Federated department store chain and the Esprit de Corps women's wear company with conspiring to cut off its supplies. There have also been occasional, subtle anti-discounter outbursts from companies like Phillips Van Heusen Co., which commented to retailers that "if you cheapen our brand, we won't sell to you...."

The pressure on manufacturers to keep everybody happy— the old clients (department stores and specialty shops) and the newer discounters with lots of hard cash—seems to be tipping in the favor of bargain-hunting off-pricers. One business writer summed up the situation humorously when he wrote: "Some manufacturers say they do not sell good to off-price stores....These manufacturers are called fibbers." In other words, it's a retail free-for-all that aids and abets the bargain hunter's search for cut-rate perfection.

But canny, practical consumers aren't waiting for Van Heusen shirts, or any other branded clothing that isn't on the racks *now.* Why should they? Bert Pulitzer, Ron Chereskin, Calvin Klein, Ralph Lauren, Adrienne Vittadini, Albert Nippon, Hardie Amies, Fila, Pauline Trigere, Salvatore Ferragamo, Betsey Johnson, Jhane Barnes, Willi Smith, Harve Bernard, Liz Claiborne, Perry Ellis, Villager, Evan Picone, Nino Cerutti, Ship 'n Shore, London Fog, Diane von Furstenberg, Members Only, Jordache, Ann Klein, Giorgio Sant'Angelo, Yves Saint Laurent, Pierre Cardin, Geoffrey Beene, Oscar de la Renta, Misty Harbor, Luba, Cacharel, Egon von Furstenberg and many other widely respected designer brands are seen in off-price establishments, and not just in one size, or as a fleeting come-on. I know, because I've seen them all.

Ever wonder how an off-pricer manages to institute savings that seem amazing? Sometimes when I'm up to my elbows in the bargain shopping trenches, I'm overcome with profound respect for the person who had the foresight to create this bargain in my paws that might have been bought in Saks or Sakowitz, only it wasn't.

Off-pricers buy most goods from the manufacturer, just as department stores do. Only the process is different—a little more democratic. Department stores insist, when placing their orders, on so-called "markdown" money from manufacturers, dollars *the manufacturer pays a store* as a sort of insurance. Markdown money assures the store a decent profit margin on merchandise even if it is eventually reduced in price. Off-pricers are not eligible for markdown money.

Department stores are also notoriously slow about paying their outstanding bills to manufacturers. The big off-pricers, on the other hand, in exchange for paying huge sums of cash up front for huge amounts of merchandise, receive up-front discounts on these goods, up to 30 percent, sometimes more.

Don Rowlett and Stu Moldow, who run California's more than two dozen Ross "dress for less" stores, explained the modus operandi of their business as follows: "We never ask for a markdown allowance and we never ask for an advertising

In many off-price stores you are likely to find all pants, or shirts, or dresses, or sweaters grouped together for easy access. Don't be intimidated by those long aisles; it almost always ends up being easier to find what you want. (Photo by Joan Tedeschi)

allowance. We never ask for return privileges.... The key to our business is turnover.... Our customer wants to stretch her wardrobe and she comes to us because she is going to get more bang for the buck from us."

The discounter passes on the savings to the customer and keeps in-store expenses to a minimum. Due to the traditionally generous markup on clothing (a department store buying a coat from the manufacturer for $100 will put it out on the floor for $200), the off-pricer still manages to clear a decent profit for himself. "If we buy a garment for $10 we will sell it for $16. A department store will get $21 for the same sweater," is the way one off-pricer explained it.

Mike Green, a fashion buyer for the large April-Marcus buying service that supplies off-price stores such as the Clothing Clearance Centers located in cities in California and Illinois, told me how he picked up 1,000 Mongolian cashmere sport coats and sold them at a price department stores simply couldn't have afforded.

First, he bought a load of quality overstock fabric, paying $117 up front for a manufacturer to whip them into men's sport coats. The price was $38 *less* than the normal wholesale price. In turn, April-Marcus offered the coats for as much as $255 in various stores it supplies. Department stores would have had to charge customers $350 for the same coats.

"Today," Mike Green says succinctly between phone calls from eager manufacturers willing to sell to off-pricers even while protesting that they won't, "bargains are a business. They're not a dirty word like they used to be. In a deal between manufacturer and buyer today it's a matter of who has the money to pay for the merchandise and when. Manufacturers still choose their associations, and some of them remain loyal to traditional accounts. But after all is said and done, they've all got their own outlets, their basements and sub-basements. For them, it's a form of profit to be paid up front, instead of later. Bargains are... the word is *legitimate* now."

The most important aspect of off-price apparel acquisition is that the best of these stores and chains react fast, fast, fast in the marketplace. No hestitating about orders as department stores traditionally do. Mike Green says "yes" to a shirt manufacturer after contemplating an order for a minute or two. Otherwise, the shirts would go elsewhere, the bargain would be lost to somebody else's "basement."

San Francisco-based Ross Stores claim to connect up to 1,000 top labels, including Dior, St. Laurent, Blass, Picone and Givenchy. They're one of the many off-price concerns that no longer must slash the labels out of the clothing they stock. Many off-pricers are finding these labels the best kind of publicity available; even if in exchange for the privilege of carrying new, in-season inventory they may be contractually prohibited by a designer or manufacturer from advertising the label in any way other than hanging it on the rack for consumers to see. Ross buyer Karen Selness explains: "The labels you see in Ross, you can see in department stores. We want to prove to you that we're saving you money (20-60 percent generally). If they don't see the label anywhere, how do they know a garment was $60.00 and they're getting it for . . . $29.95?"

Precisely. Although it's sometimes fun to speculate about an item's true designer affiliation, it's much nicer to be told outright. The fact that so many off-pricers now do give that information tells you immediately that this miraculous new addition to retailing has come of age.

Yet, as the off-price boom continues, it will take more rather than less consumer know-how to sort out the wheat from the chaff.

When shopping off-price, keep your eye peeled for changes that might adversely affect the low prices you seek:

Architectural Improvements. The nicer these stores begin to look and the more accessible geographically to consumers, the greater the likelihood that savings will diminish. It costs money to replace dim fixtures with fancy ones; to give away free coffee or add a service staff. And you'll be the one to pay for it.

Possible Top-Quality Merchandise Shortages. While the tenacity and growth of off-pricers has meant improved stock, many soothsayers in the retail sector predict that there just isn't enough merchandise to go around, especially now that some designers have invested in "factory-to-you" outlets. Evidence for this can be found already in the fact that often only so-so brands fill out the racks of off-price monoliths like Marshall's and Loehmann's and undoubtedly other off-prices as well. Industry analysts figure about 60 percent of the stock for the current or forthcoming season in off-price hands is brand new. You must carefully interpret the advertisements of some off-pricers that imply their product is the same as so-and-so designer's because it was made in the same factory. But are the fabric and workmanship the same? That's the question to ask.

Phoney Baloney Off-Pricers. You will find a few designer items under their roofs—usually distressed in some way, junk masquerading as quality, and some illegal designer fakes, too. Years ago, for instance, I bought a rather nice velvet skirt with an "Arthur Roberts" label. I mistook it for "Arthur Richards," a noted men's and women's suit manufacturer. Now I know better.

I'm also alternately amused and insulted by those now-widely-used Phoney Baloney store apparel tags with a space for "Original Price," another for "Our Price." With those marginal, fill-in-the-racks "brands," the so-called "original price" is meaningless, and must be taken with a grain of salt.

Cheapskate Off-Pricers. They reduce by 15 percent, maybe, and expect us to be grateful. Why you could do better in a department store! True-blue off-pricers can afford to discount at least 30 percent, often much more. It's not unusual to find apparel at less than half price.

Once you have tried off-price shopping, you'll come to appreciate the true meaning of this concept. It was made in heaven—for bargain lovers.

CHAPTER 6

Discount Department Stores

The American discount store is best defined by the trade magazine *Discount Store News* as "a departmentalized retail establishment utilizing many self-service techniques... it operates at low margins and a minimum annual volume of $1 million and is at least 10,000 square feet in size."

The discount store phenomenon is also a relatively recent one. In 1960, there were only 1,300 of these retailers in existence; now there are more than 8,500, of an average size of 64,000 square feet, with men's and women's apparel and shoes accounting for nearly 20 percent of store sales.

How do these monster-size stores fit into the bargain chic spectrum? Not quite off-pricers, and not nearly as exclusive as traditional department stores, discount department stores in the past have not been noted for the highest quality goods, nor have they sought the image. And historically the discount department store has *not* been the primary place consumers looked to stock their wardrobes. Women currently spend an average of about $80 a year on discount department store clothing.

K-Mart, Wal-Mart, Target, Venture, Bradlees, Gold Circle and other huge chains are actively seeking out designer apparel from the likes of Calvin Klein, Gloria Vanderbilt and Jordache, and offering them at fair prices. Although one discount department store flaunted a "Famous Brands for Less" logo above its women's fashion department, it wasn't meant to be a competitive nod to off-pricers.

Until recently, discount department stores were never known for fashion sense. But now, when you drive through those giant macadam parking lots to K-Mart or Gold Circle, you'll find designer apparel for adults and practical clothing for children at value-oriented prices. (Photo by Ebet Roberts)

Some people just don't enjoy shopping in these gigantic stores that seem like airplane hangars, stretching as far as the eye can see. I find the endless stretches of goods, the harsh lighting and incessant Muzak to be oddly soothing, but you couldn't get my husband in a K-Mart if you paid him. He walks in the door and his eyes glaze over. He doesn't know where to start, and, with so much to investigate, fears that this shopping excursion will never end. I prefer discount department stores in the evening, when there aren't too many people competing for the bargains and the check-out lines located in the front of most stores are relatively short. As I've said before, a bargain becomes less and less of a *real* bargain the longer you waste precious time standing in line waiting to pay for it.

Discount department stores offer a wide choice of merchandise and generally shy away form close-outs, irregulars and special purchase items, even those carrying famous names. These stores prefer private label or relatively unknown label names manufactured in the same factories as better-known brands. Some of the time, even now, the merchandise continues to be on the fringe of quality. This is because discount department stores have remained loyal to faithful clientele originally attracted to the basic, no nonsense low-priced clothing that was their stock-in-trade for a long time. A portion of this no-frills merchandise still remains.

But younger, trendier shoppers, are also being courted, and the result is a surprising diversity of well-made, relatively inexpensive fashion-forward clothing, as well as a wide variety of clothes for kids.

Bargain hunters *can* find good deals at discount department stores, especially on fashion-forward "gear" and sportswear type clothing. Usually manufactured in the Far East, even when it's *not* reduced discount department store apparel stock of this type usually retails for under $25. But when the sales commence, discount department stores can't be beat, not only for "name brand" but for lesser-known brand apparel as well.

Following the markdowns is extremely profitable for the discount department store bargain hunter. But the problem is that anybody who has grown up shopping primarily in such stores may not be able to spot quality. The fact is that discount department stores price the junk at just about the same level as the good stuff. An educated consumer can avoid the tacky synthetics and ineptly executed "knock-downs" of designer clothing, while taking advantage of the quality items on the same racks. By monitoring a favorite local store's "Flash" or "Blue Light" sales, where prices plummet for an hour, a wealth of genuine discounts can be found—though it's doubtful a *bargain chic* follower would be able to build an entire wardrobe on the offerings of discount department stores.

I've also discovered that some discount department stores, such as Gold Circle, are apt to have better-made merchandise if the chain is owned by a large retail conglomerate—Federated, in this case—which through a central buying office may be able to direct *the same goods* to traditional department stores *and* discount department stores. I once found children's winter vests in Gold Circle for about half the price of Abraham & Straus, a more upscale member of the Federated family. (In the "Kids' Clothes" chapter I'll tell you more about how discount department stores can help dress your kids up to *bargain chic* standards.)

Since I worked twenty summers ago in a discount department store keeping the merchandise folded, the selling concept hasn't changed. Consumers are still on their own, but in the best of these stores greater emphasis on fashion and quality has greatly improved their image.

Today, a number of large regional discount department stores, including Caldor (Connecticut), Hills (Massachusetts), Danners (Indiana), Grand Central (Nevada), G.C. Murphy (Pennsylvania) and Jamesway (New Jersey) are competing head-to-head with national chains. Both camps covet respectibility and, in their fight for patronage, prices inevitably come down, making discount department stores another *bargain chic* domain.

"Odd Lots and Schlocks" —In the early 1960s, when the original discount department stores opened, they weren't much to look at: vast macadam parking lots outside, vast linoleum floors inside and low-priced apparel you couldn't expect to last forever—or a month even. Since these stores have continually upgraded, it's only natural that others would fill the gap. They stock what I call schlock—a mishmash of junk unceremoniously amassed from here and there and thrown onto overflowing tables. (Hangers? Who ever heard of them?)

Where they get the stuff nobody knows. The schlock merchants are real scavengers, always on the scene when other stores close their doors for the last time after bankruptcy or fire, eagerly prowling factories here and abroad for leftover material or finished goods that nobody wants. One professor of schlock told me that he once bought a huge pile of triangular-shaped cuttings for almost nothing and had them made into ladies bikini underpants. There's one shop in lower Manhattan which actually stocks ripped Arrow shirts. The challenge, if you're up to it, is to find one that isn't very badly ripped. This place even has clothes with mold. (Even the schlock trade has its lower end.)

But a number of stores are appearing in the marketplace, including New York's Odd Lot Trading Company, Big Deal$, Odd Jobs Trading, and Weber's Clearance Centers, which are doing a better job finding and selling clothes in the gray area between "odd lots" and "last year's" and holey, moldy bargains. These no-nonsense establishments are amusing and serious business too. Last year I picked up a Giorgio Armani 100 percent linen, sleeveless summer dress unceremoniously clumped with other designer samples in a bin. Of course, there's no trying on unless you do it in the middle of an aisle when nobody's looking, but for $4 (original price of $80 still visible) I took the chance. The year before, I came across some lovely Betsey Johnson cotton knit dresses for $15, down from nearly $100. And sometimes, when you peel off the flimsy cellophane bags that protect the jersey shirts in these places you find decent cotton or cotton blend garments that look 100 percent better when you remove them from their schlock environment—and that's because they are actually very well made. If a department store had them pressed and placed on hangers they'd cost $8 or more, not $2.99.

Schlock shopping takes dedication—it's definitely not for everybody—but the payoffs are substantial. "Many off-price and discount stores haven't the greatest ambiance, anyway," says bargain columnist Josette Serlin, who takes pride in her ability to pluck big bargains from the schlock bins in Los Angeles. "I'd just as soon go for cement floors and cinder block walls—the freight liquidation places that are just a mess to look at but fabulous for bargains. To do it, you have to be turned on by the *adventure* of shopping. I once found some Norma Kamali capes for $5 that literally had fallen off the freight train somewhere and were rerouted to a warehouse."

The merchandise is never stable, so you never go the schlock route for specific items. Buying is pure impulse depending entirely on whether the goods are cheap enough. They usually are. Shopping the schlocks is an acquired taste. Newspaper advertisements for Big Deal$ take a tongue-in-cheek approach characteristic of rock bottom bargain centers, boasting "Best Ever" deals on "salvage, insurance losses, bankruptcies, manufacturers' ($ problems) stock. Anyway, anywhere we can get quality stuff cheap. We take chances. You never have to!"

They're right, you don't have to take a chance; they offer a seven-day-money-back guarantee on such "99 percent perfect" merchandise as Levis and Guess jeans, sportswear by Diffusion and Inwear. This clothing is available at 60 percent off retail or more because "a water pipe broke at a 'super exclusive' Madison Avenue shop." In good fun, Big Deal$ asks customers, "*Do you* pay more for pre-wash?"

CHAPTER 7

Boutiques

In the old-fashioned specialty shops the proprietor knew your name and size and just what you wanted even before you did. The specialty clothing shops that lined Main Street, U.S.A., their names in boldly looped script above the door, seem almost prehistoric now. In some ways that's too bad. When we shop giant department, off-price and discount department stores it's almost impossible to develop a lasting relationship with the staff, and the style of these stores can't compare to what used to be.

Ladies specialty shops aspired to elegance and style, men's to a private club atmosphere, even when the neighborhood where they were located was a trifle on the decline. In these establishments a woman or man could expect undivided attention, expert tailoring and quality clothing. And they got it. People weren't looking for bargains.

Today boutiques have replaced most specialty stores. They come in all levels of *chic*, from the spiffy shops on Rodeo Drive in Los Angeles and Manhattan's Madison Avenue where the currency is glamor and the aim exclusivity, to more down-to-earth mall shops with interchangeable names and merchandise.

If markdowns remain something of an afterthought in the upscale specialty boutiques of America, the owners of these stores nevertheless do capitulate a bit to the new national mania for discounted clothing.

I was recently led to a very lovely new privately owned suburban specialty boutique nestled into a hill adjacent to an exquisite old barn converted into a stylish restaurant. The window sparkled with pretty things that were evidently of the finest quality. I balked at the thought of entering. Sometimes a store seems to be screaming out the awful truth: Don't bother. No bargains here. I almost turned on my heels and left, but something told me to take the chance, check it out. As I brushed by the rack of silk blouses next to the front door I saw a $220 price tag. My throat tightened. I browsed politely but wondered, "What am I doing here? I adore lovely clothes as much as the next person, but a $220 blouse? Not a necessity just now."

Then, partially obscured in the rear, I noticed a small "Sale" sign and made a well-mannered bee line toward it. The sales lady said, as I picked delicately through the rack, "Anything you see here is 70 percent off." She was very cheerful about it, so I went to work, sizing up the spoils.

That day I found an exquisite silk blouse reduced from $129 to $37 and a linen/cotton blend dress with a comparable markdown, $135 to $38.

The manager, who happened to be the mother of the owner, explained that some of the store's most up-to-date fashion items wouldn't sell even at a reduction in that part of the country. But, she said, it was important for the shop to reflect the newest styles, even if it meant marking down some apparel at the end of the season. She looked delighted that *somebody* was giving that terrific blouse with football shoulders a loving home, and I was just as pleased to adopt it.

As with many small specialty shops the sale was not widely advertised, except to a select mailing list of regular customers. It turned out nearly everything in the shop was reduced by 20 percent, and the manager very willingly told me when further store-wide reductions would take place. She added me to the mailing list.

There's a pride that the owners of such shops typically project. They're in touch with the leading fashion showrooms

Most boutiques simply can't stock the variety of apparel available in department, discount and off-price stores, but it's the rare boutique that doesn't provide a good deal on one or two coveted brand names. (Photo by Ebet Roberts)

and always on the prowl for engaging new work by up-and-coming designers, but they also know precisely what regular customers want from fashion. It's as close as retailing comes these days to a family connection, and is diametrically opposed to the anonymous fend-for-yourself atmosphere cultivated by the vast fashion caverns in which many of us usually shop. While for bargain hunters these little places never can be a major source of mark-downs, the select, high-quality merchandise, carefully reflecting the taste of the owner, can be a source of inspiration and occasional purchase for a fashion bargain wardrobe.

Get to know the manager and owner. Drop in just to admire the apparel. Talk fashion first, sales and bargains later. Look good when you go. Your refreshing perspetive and knowledge of style and trends may well ingratiate you to the owner. When that's accomplished, you'll be in line for some super savings.

In another boutique category are those trendy little places with small tufts of dresses, blouses, sweaters and sometimes shoes, and a few bored individuals sitting around watching your every move. I inevitably feel self-conscious when I shop these boutiques, because I'm one of those people who prefers a bit of anonymity while making fashion *and* bargain decisions. Also, in these less fashionable boutiques there's seldom enough stock on any one visit to have a real impact on a wardrobe, enough selection to find an item or two to fill it out.

Many small boutiques tend to exhibit a similar lack of distinction. The chief reason is that boutiques are usually independently owned and operated and survival hinges on the sale of middle-of-the-road, medium-priced apparel. The fact is that many boutiques are only marginally successful. You can often tell by the stagnant decor and the seemingly arbitrary pricing systems. It's not unusual for boutiques to stock one or two known designers and a bigger selection of merchandise that makes up for brand anonymity by being flashy, colorful and not too outrageously priced.

Boutique shopping necessarily means making the rounds but it can be fun. A visit to a half-dozen boutiques on a lazy afternoon can also fill you in on some of the most fashion-forward directions. By the time you finish browsing it's almost impossible to figure out where you saw what without having written it down. Travel with a pad and pencil.

Chances of finding an enormously appealing bargain in such stores is limited. A small shopkeeper is not about to mark down goods if he can eke out a sale at full price.

That means instead of the relatively fresh bargains and "special purchase" items you'd find for the same prices in a department store, in boutiques you'll likely see last season's leftovers on sale racks, along with distressed merchandise—sweaters ripped, pulled or misshapen by hangers, pants that aren't quite the right shape, and other marginals, along with fad fashion that just didn't catch on. The inevitable boutique pilgrimage you must make in order to find just what you need, translates into more time-consuming shopping than if you were *doing* a full-service department store or a larger off-price establishment. It's not easy on the feet or the memory bank.

Take note of still another type of boutique in existence which does not usually win you over with a trendy atmosphere—mesmerizing love ballads piped in over quadraphonic sound systems, hip young salespeople or fetchingly designed windows.

In my book, they're called "hole-in-the-walls," and to shop them is to experience bare-bones consumerism. Offshoots of New York's Lower East Side discount fashion outlets, these "holes" can now be found all over the country, on side streets, in old-fashioned shopping center strips, and sometimes even in private homes: wherever there's somebody who knows where to get the goods.

The hole-in-the-walls are often mini-off-pricers. Some of them thrive solely on the sale of sample goods in specific sizes. Others have connections with designers who are relieved that

Their signs are faded. Sometimes all external identifying marks seem to have disappeared. But inside these hole-in-the wall boutiques the identifying marks are obvious: bargains galore on branded merchandise. (Photo by Ebet Roberts)

overstock can be quietly removed to such places. If you've ever frequented a hole-in-the-wall boutique you'll probably notice the owner stumbling in on occasion, weighted down by a motley selection of styles and sizes, irregulars, seconds and incredibly perfect stuff, too. It may be an unceremonious way to deliver goods, but it's quintessential bargain hunter's territory. Precisely *because* the owner has obtained the goods without ceremony he's eager to sell it that way. He may even want to bargain with you.

To sum up, here is my seasoned advice to get the best out of boutique shopping:

- Get to know the owner or manager. Boutiques are usually so small that the person working the cashier or the floor is the person in charge. Unless a boutique is on a main thoroughfare, working in one can be a lonely profession. These people need to talk, whether it be about clothes or the weather.

- If you're particularly impressed with the merchandise, say so. Once you've become a good customer, ask some questions about markdown policy. Many boutiques have one or two excellent wholesale sources they can count on for designer bargains. While the general stock may not all be discounted, a boutique owner needs to have discounted drawing cards, usually the fashions of a few designers with whom he has the inside track. I remember being in a tiny boutique in my neighborhood when the owner came in, his arms full to bursting with about 50 Liz Claiborne dresses he'd just finagled from somewhere. I was understandably curious. The saleslady told me that her boss could be expected to return with similar riches every *other* Thursday morning. Their best customers, she told me, knew this and were sure to arrive Thursdays during lunch hour to sort through the latest acquisitions.

- When you purchase $100 or more, you may be able to swing further reductions. Maybe you'd love that suede jacket, but can't see your way to parting with another $50. I've known hole-in-the-wall entrepreneurs to immediately lower the price. They survive on cash business and would rather have your payment now and the garment off the rack than not. That means you must have the courage to bargain $5, $10, maybe $15 off the total price of your purchases. All you have to do is say: "Would you consider taking (name your price but expect the proprietor to bargain back)? I really love the clothes, but I just don't have enough on me right now." You'd be surprised how effective this tactic can be!

I've always been a wary boutique shopper because I prefer making my own decisions at my own pace. There's nothing worse than the eagle eye of a boutique owner or salesperson as you try to be casual about browsing. There's an especially nice boutique in my neighborhood where I browse every few weeks, but rarely buy because, though the clothes are superb, the prices are just too high, even with markdowns. By now, the owner surely knows me, though he acts as if he doesn't. He's probably muttering, "There she is again." I'll admit to being slightly embarrassed. But one of these days I'll catch him in the middle of a surprising sale, and I *will* buy. And I already know that whatever it is, it will be boutique-special.

CHAPTER 8

Outlets

As you speed down the highway the giant, classically worded billboard comes into view: "Take Exit 15 to the Sweater Outlet. 50,000 sweaters direct from factory to you." The sign is tantalizing to a bargain hunter, and those who take the time to veer off at Exit 15 know the pleasure of a real factory outlet nestled at the backdoor of a plant, operating without fanfare or decorative flourishes, but stuffed with merchandise.

In the early days of outlets, the merchandise was usually irregulars or seconds piled every which way in bins. For the tenacious bargain maven, however, rummaging around for a factory outlet gem has always been a part of the fun.

Relatively pure forms of outlets still exist. I've jumped into some of the bins at the Champion Knitwear outlet in a suburb near Rochester, N.Y., and rolled around with thousands of T-shirts stamped with college athletic department names and slogans. And some new outlet centers are situated within pre-existing manufacturing complexes and textile mills.

But, for the most part, public perception of outlets as rough-and-tumble bargain-lovers' territory has been supplanted by retail stores masquerading as outlets. Too strong a word, "masquerading"? Perhaps, because these stores do offer cents-off merchandise. But they're very definitely in the retail business—not in the business of factory-to-you oddities and exceptions that dare you to buy. Among the many shops in the maze known as the Secaucus (N.J.) Outlet Center, for instance, the Chaus store has prices that are hardly on the bargain level. One shopper told me she wasn't surprised. "Why do you think they have that big sign out front that says 'Retail'?" she asked.

The eighties are the era of *outlet malls*, which combine the beauty of self-contained mall or strip shopping with the lure of deep discounts. They attract several different kinds of shops—those operated by manufacturers which carry only their own brands; those which are off-price divisions of larger retail operations; and individual entrepreneurs who, instead of running boutiques or off-price stores, have opted for an outlet-style pricing system.

The Secaucus Outlet Center is one of the fastest-growing. In 1978 there were 14 stores; now there are more than 50. Designers and manufacturers like Liz Claiborne and Henry Grethel boldly advertise their names on the doors of their spacious "outlets" while other stores, stocking assorted designer merchandise obtained in exchange for the promise of anonymity, operate behind unmarked doors. Neither a mall nor a shopping center, the Secaucus outlet scene utilizes existing factory space. But outlet industry observers predict more centers with upscale looks. These include the forthcoming Fashion Plaza, also in New Jersey, with a characteristically massive 400,000 square feet of store space for 70 stores, and the future Outlet Bazaar in Yorktown Heights, New York, which will feature a central atrium and two floors of stores. Even the new outlet centers situated in historic buildings, such as Baltimore's Outlet at Harbor Exchange, and Richmond's Main Street Station, a renovated Chessie System railroad stop, will hardly look like one outlet I used to frequent in Upstate New York: To get to that one you had to ride a rickety freight elevator.

Outlet mall shopping is fun—you know *everything* in the store is always "on sale"—and, as such, is the most seductive form of bargain hunting. When busfuls of shoppers pour through the door, their wallets bulging with cash and charge cards, the pressure point rises and you, too, feel it's time to spend. Patricia Scotto runs a service called Luxury Theater and Dining, which now books one and two-day bargain shopping binges to the

Outlet centers and malls like this one in suburban Rochester, N.Y., are shooting up all over the country. They run the gamut from no-frills warehouse-type outlets to lavish landmark renovations. No matter what the look, the idea is to offer branded merchandise at daily discounts. (Photo by Ebet Roberts)

Secaucus outlet center. "They come to spend money—lots and lots of it," she told me. "One busful spent $12,000. Grandmothers buy presents for every grandchild. Yuppies come, educated young couples who still aren't making enough to buy the most expensive clothes at full price—but they must look as if they do— and they leave with piles of purchases." Leave it to canny developers like the people in Kansas City, Mo., who are building the $9 million Great Midwest Factory Outlet Mall right next door to two big theme parks. How could *anybody* pass it up?

In Patricia Scotto's view, outlet buying is contagious, though prices, even at a discount, remain relatively steep. "A typical item would be a handbag that was $300 in Saks Fifth Ave. You can get it for $169 in Secaucus," says Scotto. The question people have to ask themselves is, "Do I need a $169 handbag?"

The financial catch at outlet malls featuring designer-quality fashion is that they rarely sell anything *below* cost while department stores and off-pricers are often forced or willing to do so.

In a Harve Bernard outlet, for instance, if the "Original Price" reads $300, the hungry bargain hunter ponders whether the revised $225 price tag is a real bargain. (Having bought a Bernard winter coat reduced from $300 to $99 in a women's specialty boutique, I would think twice.)

"We make a profit, just a lower profit," is how one outlet mall entrepreneur put it. And it's not hard to do on clothing which department stores traditionally sell for double the factory price—their standard 100 percent markup. At outlets it might be a 50 percent markup or less. But if the coat's "original price" is $400, you'll virtually never find it for $100 or $59 at an outlet the way you might at a real sale.

Designer/manufacturers who operate outlet stores also engage in creative markdowns that sometimes seem better than they really are. If you're a follower of Liz Claiborne, Ann Klein, Evan Picone, Bill Blass, Calvin Klein—take your pick—viewing a vast array of their current fashion under one roof may be enough to convince you that the tag that reads

ORIGINAL PRICE: $47
OUR PRICE: $38

is a thrill enough to cause you to buy. But in *bargain chic* terms, 20 percent off isn't enough; 50 percent and we'll consider it!

As in any other shopping mode, when making the outlet rounds be familiar with how much the clothing you like *really* costs, as well as the quality of workmanship. Mesmerized by the designer mystique which outlet malls and strips foster, it's sometimes easy for a shopper to forget that there's more to clothing than the label inside.

As you can see from the current town-by-town list of outlet malls and centers in the "Resource" section of this book, this is a burgeoning shopping form. Here are my suggestions for making the outlet experience a good one for you:

1. Find out about the outlet center before you go. Some of them are stretched out over miles and you'll waste a lot of time figuring out where to go if you wait until you get there.

2. If you're eager to buy, bring cash. Many outlets do not take checks or credit cards.

3. Be prepared for communal dressing rooms and every kind of basic off-price decor. Travel light. There will sometimes be no chairs and no salespeople to watch your bags and coats.

4. Find out whether the outlet you will be visiting is designed for children. Unlike traditional malls with wide, all-weather public areas and in-door diversions (movie theaters and eating places), some malls are no more than factories linked together by a theme—saving money. We took our children shopping to one outlet center and were lucky to find some shriveled up hot dogs at an outdoor stand for lunch. It may even be a good idea to bring a picnic.

5. Remember that the outlet shopping experience is so new that it is attracting huge masses of people on weekends and holidays. If you don't like crowds, consider a visit on a weekday.

My final word on outlet mall shopping is "beware." The millions of dollars developers and retailers are investing in this new shopping form means *somebody* has to pay for it. Know before you travel the outlet circuit that you've got to be very smart about prices and brands; if you are not, you won't save much money. As veteran retailing writer Eric Peterson wrote recently in *Stores* magazine, it's vital to know "where conventional [retailing] ends and off-price begins" in the world of outlet malls. When you do, make the most of it by celebrating *bargain chic.*

CHAPTER 9

Vintage, Thrift, Resale, Rummage, Garage, Second-Hand

Bargains in Someone Else's Clothes

Some people only shop second hand. Let them tell you how:

"I go down the aisle slowly. I pick out anything that's wool and cotton. I bypass the polyester. I don't stop and look at every garment on every hanger. It would take an age and it wouldn't be worth it. You can see the miserable things a mile away. It's funny how they stick out, especially when they're used. A bargain is only a bargain if it's true quality and that goes for second-hand, too, even if the price is only 50 cents. Other than the amazing clothes you find in thrift shops, the great thing is that you *can* make mistakes and they cost almost nothing. You just give them back if they don't work."

***

"The best bargains are those where the seller doesn't know the value, has no appreciation for its fine points. You *do* see it, and you pluck it off the rack. Sometimes, if you're traveling, you'll see stuff that would be extremely valuable to you at home, in another climate. But the person or organization selling it doesn't see that worth. I bought wool suits in resale and second-hand shops in Hawaii that people who'd resettled there didn't need. I paid a few dollars each for these Saks and Joseph Magnin and Sakowitz suits which were in perfect condition, real bargains."

***

"You can't be fancy if you're going after somebody else's leftovers. There's a place called Hohenwall, Tennessee, where the dry cleaning stores turn over all their unclaimed clothing. They put these bales of clean but used clothes on the floor. You jump in and pick up what you can along with a crowd of other people. Then you go off into a corner, if you can find one, and see what you've come up with. They charge you almost nothing for this service. Sometimes you get something incredibly good that you can really wear. The problem is that it can get frightening being there. Everybody goes crazy after the bargain. There's so much pressure to get something. One woman begged me, 'Please, let me have that.' I wouldn't give it to her. Now, every time I look at it, I feel guilty."

***

"I went to a garage sale. The lady was cleaning out possessions from 30 years ago, when she'd gotten married. I found some clothes I liked. Some were potentially worth a lot of money. I let her set the price. She seemed apologetic when she asked for $1 for each item. You don't know if you can keep a straight face. These kinds of bargains are one of a kind."

***

"I like to simulate, to see something in an expensive place and try to duplicate it second-hand. I bought an expensive instantly recognizable designer skirt in a resale shop for 25 cents. Anybody who knows designer clothes could tell it was expensive, and who designed it. I wore it with a little boy's T-shirt that cost 50 cents. People kept asking, 'Where did you get that top?' It was my private joke. I had made that shirt expensive by juxtaposing it with something that was, even if the skirt cost me almost nothing.

"To be an effective bargain hunter you need imagination. The thrift shops stimulate that in me, as well as the quality which just isn't as available elsewhere. Where *can* you find the gabardine, silk, crepe de chine, the beautiful quality, new, without spending a fortune? I'm not afraid to look for the clothes I want. 'If it ain't got that swing'... well, it's not in my wardrobe. That's why I do it all second-hand."

***

"I only go to those thrift shops run by charities. You can get *brand new clothing* donated by major department stores. The tags are still on them. The thrift shop marks it down by at least half, sometimes by 75 percent. Part of the enjoyment for me is going through the piles that they put any which way on tables. You see all these designer labels sticking out—Kamali, Ellis, Klein, Bernard, Kenzo—I mean, *the very best* end up on these tables. Hundred-dollar blouses are mixed up in paper boxes and brown bags with $200 suits. It's always a very quiet atmosphere, as if the aura of the charity is keeping us all from busting a gut from bargain euphoria."

***

"In Los Angeles, the disposable culture prevails in fashion, too. There are so many social events and people can't wear the same things over and over. But this clothing is too expensive to discard, so it goes to resale shops that sell it in excellent condition, at up to one-third the original retail price. This is incredible merchandise, really the *top* fashion. All people have to do is to be able to change their mentality to accept wearing somebody else's clothes. But these are great places for self-admitted clothes horses who want the best."

***

In this chapter about buying other people's clothing and accessories, I've let other people do the talking, but let me say that rummaging at rummage sales and in people's garages and musty apartments, picking through the piles at the Volunteers of America, Salvation Army and the vast number of charity thrift shops that exist throughout the country, and finding prizes on the burgeoning re-sale market, is an acquired taste.

Frankly, I didn't used to like it. But the more one makes the rounds, the more convincing the pastime of second-hand shopping becomes. Having found so many wonderful buys this way, I now find myself working my weekend schedule around local bazaars and being unable to pass by a thrift shop without checking it out. Today, just before writing these words, I found a brand-new, made-in-Italy, 100 percent wool sweater for my daughter at an apartment sale in my neighborhood. Price: 25 cents.

Remember the following tips when you feel like rummaging:

- Though resale and vintage shops generally have fixed prices, most other second-hand places encourage bargaining. If you just don't want to spend what's printed on the price tag, offer what you can, preferably in a self-confident tone of voice. Be prepared to compromise your perfect price.

- Look to rummage-, thrift-, and garage-type second-hand sales to stock children's wardrobes. If your own neighborhood doesn't have much to offer, check the Sunday classifieds of your local paper, regular newspaper "bargain" columns, and community bulletin boards at laundramats and supermarkets. Look for best-quality merchandise at church and synagogue bazaars in upscale areas.

- If you find an item that nobody but you recognizes as priceless, don't hesitate to purchase it as cheaply as possible. That's part of the game. Without calling attention to yourself, buy it quickly and enjoy—without guilt.

- If you're planning to attend a country auction, don't bid blindly on an item if you haven't had a chance to examine it closely.

- Women should peruse the men's departments of thrift and second-hand shops for soft, well-worn, oversized clothing.

- Find scads of terrific old buttons and lacy bric-a-brac for accessorizing at country antique shows and city rummage sales.

- Don't buy injured apparel second-hand unless you love to mend. Often, the material is too fragile and aged to withstand any kind of tampering.

- Discover which local charitable thrift shops work with major department stores as regular dumping grounds for quality *new* clothing.

- When you buy used, be very sure you know the value of the merchandise. Don't be conned by persuasive salespeople into paying for a so-called "antique." Not everything is.

CHAPTER 10

Mail Order

If you compute a bargain on the basis of the time it takes to locate a quality item, then mail order shopping should be part of your scheme. Personally, I almost never shop by mail because, though I'm spending money, the process conducted from my home lacks the tactile stimulation I enjoy when I'm in a store, sniffing out bargains. But a lot of you must be doing it, because industry statistics put catalog sales at nearly $50 billion a year.

Thousands of catalogs now exist, covering the fashion and price spectrum. Every year, J. C. Penney and Sears churn out more than two dozen each, and, of course, Spiegel puts out its gargantuan seasonal catalogs that are virtual department stores in print.

Increasingly, the aim of mail order is to bring exclusivity into our homes. Otherwise, we could drive to the nearest mall and buy the same merchandise, and probably less expensively. So J. C. Penney can sell its new Halston and Ann Klein lines in its catalogs, as well as the Sesame Street clothing it markets exclusively. Spiegel has upgraded substantially by introducing designers like Normal Kamali to its catalog clientele. If you live in the hinterlands, where Halston and Kamali aren't always available in stores, then mail order can do the trick.

For children, some catalogs stock 100 percent, old-fashioned cotton clothing which is simply impossible to find elsewhere; and for larger-sized men and women, catalogs bring the clothing they need to them without the need for traipsing from store to store for what usually is limited selection. Then there are the novelty catalogs, stocking original T-shirts and other items which are never sold in stores.

But for my money, mail order has more negatives than positives, unless you really hate shopping. Here are my reasons why:

1. Though mail order saves time at the outset, if you don't like what you've purchased, you must repackage the item and send it back.

2. Pretty pictures on models don't always mean the merchandise looks good on you. It's hard to judge the quality of catalog garments and whether they'll actually fit.

3. Though many mail order houses are reputable, the possibility exists that, after your check is cashed, you'll never see what you paid for. That's happened to me twice after I was too lazy to check with the Direct Mail/Marketing Association to see whether the companies with whom I was dealing were on the up and up.

4. Some merchandise—swimsuits, underwear—is not returnable.

5. Some companies demand that you sign for goods upon receipt. That's fine, but if you're not home or available in the office, back goes the package to the post office, and you've got to get in your car to pick it up.

Here's a short list of some mail order houses which specialize in cut-rate fashion.

Banana Republic
P. O. Box 77133
San Francisco, CA 94107

Chadwick's of Boston
One Chadwick Place
Boston, Mass. 02072

Company B Store
Dept. B
1205 South 7th St.
La Crosse, Wisconsin 54601

Cotton Dreams
999 Laredo Lane
Box 1261
Sebastian, Florida 32958

Eastern Mountain Sports
One Vose Farm Road
Peterboro, NH 03438

Grand Finale
P.O. Box 340257
Farmer's Branch, Texas 75234

Land's End
Land's End Lane
Dodgeville, Wisc. 53533

Mother's Work (maternity)
P.O. Box 40121
Philadelphia, Pa. 19106

Roaman's (half and larger sizes)
Saddle Brook, New Jersey 07662

Additional mail-order ideas can be found in the book
Clothing-By-Mail Catalogue, by Sarah Gallick, published by
New American Library.

CHAPTER 11

Accessories

There are two kinds of accessories—those that last and those designed not to. A bargain chic wardrobe should include some of each.

Accessories are outfit finishers. Although one stylish soul I know built her wardrobe around five outrageously expensive Elsa Peretti bracelets in red and black and one Peretti belt, most of us approach accessories the other way around: We assemble the clothing and then we highlight it with jewelry, belts, shoes, bags. Discovering the right *look* for a particular day and season has as much to do with these accoutrements as it does with the clothing itself.

Recently a friend of mine who isn't a shopper or a fashion plate called to say she'd purchased an elegant outfit for an important professional dinner. But she was stumped about earrings, necklaces, bracelets, shoes. "I don't *own* any," she remarked plaintively.

On my advice, she made the rounds of various bargain jewelry shops and department store costume jewelry departments, but the task was overwhelming and after a day in the trenches she came home empty-handed. So I opened my jewel box and selected a dozen pair of earrings of every variety, some necklaces and bracelets, and sent them over.

My friend tried on each while wearing her new clothes, and, as she tells it, the experience was no less than a *revelation*. She couldn't get over *what a difference* one pair of earrings made. In a moment's time she passed from blasé shopper satisfied with the bare necessities to one who appreciates the finishing touches, the elements of style that transform an outfit into a statement.

For a long time I didn't realize how lucky I was as a teenager to have received presents of brooches, necklaces and bracelets, including some antiques. I've built upon this collection by ferreting out earrings at country fairs, next-to-new sales and church bazaars where classic costume jewelry is often sold for pennies—and purchasing the occasional "real thing" when it appears. I often mix baubles with genuine stones and metals, and match finery with fad.

The life-support of my jewelbox (a terrific, multi-leveled tool kit) are my trademark accessories—the bold, beautiful, timeless antique pin and bracelet originally purchased in Mexico by my father and given to my mother more than 40 years ago. Often, I wear them together; sometimes, just the wide, silvery bracelet. Always, the dimension they provide to an outfit is inestimable. And on those occasions when these accessories are too dramatic, I call upon the very simple silver chain which I wear all the time and on which hangs the tiniest diamond chip, in a setting which, nevertheless, manages to suggest a larger stone. Earrings, belts, scarves come next.

Fashion consultant Alice Meyer believes that the right accessories "make clothes talk," and should have "impact." In her book *Clotheswise* Meyer and co-author Clara Pierre argue that accessories should never be considered just "wonderful 'little' items—the kind you fall in love with, pay a pretty price for, and watch spending their lives on your shelves."

These fashion accessories—"addables" as Meyer and Pierre call them—"really talk . . . when they appear over and over to announce you—when they become your very own trademark." Meyer should know. She is the friend I mentioned earlier whose own wardrobe rests securely on Peretti jewelry!

Accessories increasingly suit men too, despite the disinclination of many males to give them a try. Start with a silk scarf, one fine piece of jewelry—tie tack, distinctive ring—if

Look for accessories that can serve as your "signature," like this antique Mexican bracelet and pin. Build from them with bargain accessories available in all types of stores. (Photo by Ebet Roberts)

he's so inclined; or belts that support not only his trousers but a sense of style.

Male or female, "the idea is to choose one addable," Meyer and Pierre contend, "that says *you* to the world-at-large. It can be a certain kind of shoe, or a collection of caps, or a flower pinned to your lapel. It can even be color. Once you choose it, never be without it."

Accessories are so important, but they should also be *fun* to wear. "In some measure," says Diane Kaiser, a former editor of *Accessories* magazine, "what you buy to complement your clothes, should reflect a sense of humor. With the right accessories you can let the child in you out.

"Like clothes, accessories express *you*, but they can't do it alone," says Kaiser. "It's as much in the way you hold your shoulders, walk, and the look on your face. Finding the right accessories can be an adventure."

***

Accessorizing is, for me, one of the most enjoyable parts of constructing an outfit. When just the right "look" coalesces, there's a real feeling of achievement.

Whatever kind of bargain hunter you are, accessories are just around the corner. Here's a run-down on where to go and how to find jewelry according to *bargain chic* standards:

Department Stores—Never bypass the jewelry department, usually located on the first floor. If you like gold, buy your chains and earrings *only* at sales advertising 40 to 60 percent off. These are sold virtually year-round.

Today's inventive costume jewelry is another department store strength; they have it at every price, and are right up there with the trends. Many department stores relegate the rock-bottom bargains to one or two display cases, sometimes without much fanfare. Among the beauties you can often find are special imported items discovered in Timbuktu, or someplace equally exotic, by an adventurous buyer who later found consumers weren't quite as enthusiastic. Learn where these are and always check them out. Most department stores have smaller accessories sections on other floors, often adjoining the shoes. Additionally, some of the cutest items can be found in the girls' and teens' department. If your favorite stores maintain bargain basements, who knows what you'll find, usually in a tangled mess, on some off-the-beaten-track? Look for handbag bargains in department store shoe areas as well as the basement.

Off-Pricers—Some of the larger chains stock jewelry without fanfare, at 50 percent off for starters. I've seen such offerings with "designer" labels but not much designer inspiration to warrant the still-steep prices. Such stores, however, often have a wide selection of belts priced for *bargain chic*. Don't be afraid to get down on your hands and knees and prowl *underneath* the belt racks, if you have to, to locate that gem reduced by 90 percent. Same with scarves, socks, and hats. You never know what's under the pile until you look.

Neckwear for men and boys, priced at about 50 percent off in many off-price establishments, can easily be converted to female use. Men's socks have become nubbier and nicer and women can roll them and layer them.

Discount Department Stores and Five-and-Tens—Can't be beat for junk jewelry that makes you smile when you wear it. A dollar or two for earrings or a necklace may be too much to pay. Prowl around those little counter-top wicker receptacles holding unadvertised 2/.99 bargains. Frequent discount department stores for inexpensive summer sandals.

Tag and Rummage Sales, Flea Markets, Resale, Church Bazaars and Thrift Shops—In these unlikely places you'll find some of the best accessories of all. I'm partial to sales run by non-professionals who either don't know how much an item should cost, or are selling cheaply for the fun of it. Try bargaining with the parishioner stationed at the jewelry table, where all earrings are 25 cents, regardless of workmanship and style considerations. I've known sale mavens to sweep up a whole mound of goodies unceremoniously wrapped in a plastic bag, by offering a flat $1 or $2. The rummage route will also lead you to lovely swatches of lace, satin or velvet from old doilies, curtains and table cloths that could be used for handkerchiefs, scarves and shawls. Bargaining is *expected* in many of these venues, so don't be afraid to try it. When you get home and sort out your finds, some of which will be very old, check to make sure the earrings and pins are sturdy. If not, carefully remove the clasps, and remount using today's quick-bonding glues.

Women in search of unusual accessories shouldn't overlook what's in the men's department. Items here, such as ties and socks, are often much more reasonably priced than they would be in the women's department. (Photo by Joan Tedeschi)

Schlock Stores—The places with piles of weird closeouts—facial creams wedged next to matchbox cars, men's socks mixed up with ornate salt and pepper shakers. Who knows what you'll find in a mound of jewelry saved from destruction in a fire or a going-out-of-business sale? Schlock stores are one of the best places for the little fun baubles that you'll want to wear on a bright spring day. And some of the antiquatedly ornate, bejewelled handbags you'll see in these establishments make perfect party dress-up accessories.

At Home—Living with a man? When he isn't looking, borrow his big, bold watch, his string and bow ties and tie tacks, or roam retail store men's accessory departments for items that may well be cheaper for him than if they were made for her.

Keep your eyes open and your mood, too. You never know where a tiny treasure may appear that will perk up your old red dress!

Shoes are accessories, too. Sometimes it seems as if there are more shoe stores in existence than there are people to buy shoes. Shoes with style, a good fit, and quality workmanship—are not easy to find. But a *bargain chic* shoe lover never gives up.

Maggie Mercado, designer and executive vice-president of the Pappagallo division of U.S. Shoe Corporation, put it this way when I asked her to explain the importance of shoes: "They are one accessory that nobody can rush out of the house without, even in the midst of a crisis. No matter what else you forget to wear, you've got to have them on; once you do, they've got to be comfortable, otherwise your whole body will be affected."

So-called "discount" shoe stores are proliferating, stocking merchandise with seductively foreign labels which range in price from under $10 to $200, while in the most exclusive designer shops footwear can be found for a whopping $1000.

Although shoes of man-made materials are most common—check the bottom or inside the shoe if you're not sure of the content—it's not impossible to find 100 percent leather footwear at rock bottom prices.

"Always go for leather uppers," Mercado says, "because it's not only better for the health of the foot, but it breathes better." Mercado says leather soles are fine, but also look for synthetic bottoms "built especially for comfort and a look that can't be achieved purely in leather."

Mercado suggests building a bargain chic shoe collection based on standards purchased late in the season for a fraction of the original price. They'll be useful next year, too.

- Handsewn classic moccasins or loafers
- Flat-heeled, riding boots
- Medium heel pumps in wine, taupe, black
- Ballerina skimmer flats
- Plain white sneakers
- Patent leather pumps

Once you've got the basics, fill in with some trendier styles that amuse you and perk up specific outfits. I maintain that *bargain chic*-ers who watch sales at some of America's classic lower-priced, mass-produced shoe marts like Bakers, Shoe-Town, Fayva and Chandlers, will find suprisingly convincing leather copies of more expensively priced shoes. They won't last forever, and you wouldn't want them to. When the sales move to racks in back of the store, you'll have a ball hopping around on one foot as you look for that "blue dot" gem reduced to $3.98—or less!

And just how important is a shoe with designer imprint? Shoe industry experts told me that quality is often absent from designer shoes manufactured in small quantities or by companies licensing designer names. Often the label is merely used to lend cachet to mediocre shoes.

Recently, a "gray market" in shoe importing has developed as well, where shoes with counterfeit trademarks are being touted as the real thing. So if that "designer" shoe looks poorly made, it may be a fake, and even the retailer might not realize it.

Says Maggie Mercado: "Larger shoe companies are often able to build a greater degree of fit engineering and quality control into the product, and these shoes may be less expensive to buy precisely because they're mass produced. When you buy a pair of $300 alligator shoes you're definitely paying for the material, *not* the fit. It takes about 180 separate operations to make a shoe, and it has to end up matching the other one. A misfit can literally cripple you—at any price."

Shoes That Don't Fit Are Never a Bargain

The Footwear Council issues these important guidelines to help those who believe that how a shoe looks is more important than how it feels—until we try to walk around. Okay, so I admit I've been in this very predicament more than once!

The best time of day to shop for shoes is the afternoon, when your foot is likely to be "swollen" to its largest size. Yes, feet do swell, as many of us who have kicked off our shoes during a movie only to be unable to get them back on afterwards can attest.

Don't believe the salesperson who insists that a new pair of shoes will stretch. Fine leather shoes are apt to loosen up, but heavier leathers and synthetics probably won't. "Shoes should feel comfortable from the moment you put them on, without being stretched or broken in."

In the store try *both* shoes on, since one foot is usually larger. Then buy to fit the larger foot.

Consider length, depth and width of a shoe, and how it feels at the ball, the widest part of the foot. At the back, the shoe should have a snug feeling without digging into your foot. The counter, inside the back of the shoe, should be smoothly constructed inside and should not pinch your foot.

Make sure your toes aren't being crushed.

The insole, under your foot, inside the shoe, should be smooth, without bumps.

Make sure the last shape upon which the shoe is constructed is right for you. If not, try another brand.

Always walk around the store to make sure you can walk.

These Shoes Are Made for Walkin'

When you buy boots:

(1) make sure they're not too loose; otherwise you'll be in for skin irritations.

(2) Choose boots with zippers if you've got a high instep.

(3) Make sure there's about ½ inch in front of your longest toe, because feet tend to swell when wearing boots.

(4) Don't try on boots with thick socks if you're planning to wear them with thinner stockings.

(5) Remember that you may require a larger size when you purchase boots without heels.

(6) If knee-high boots feel tight around the leg, put them back.

(7) Make sure the inside seams in an unlined boot are flat.

(8) Look for leather boots, as synthetics tend to breath poorly.

(9) Shy away from boots with counters in the back which are so hard that while they're supporting your heel they're also destroying it.

(10) Remember that boots with stitching at the bottom may be a poor investment, for they tend to leak.

Over 200 operations are required to make a pair of boots—and up to twice as much labor as shoemaking. Boot manufacture requires special equipment and approximately six square feet of material to produce; for high-heeled boots, another six feet are needed for the inner lining.

***

A wonderful suit... dress... sweater... trousers. The perfect accessories. You're proud of your latest *bargain chic* accomplishment. You feel ready to face the world. But somehow you forgot the shoes. Never again! Thrifty-budgeting will actually allow you to spend a little more on footwear, if you must. But at all those shoe stores out there, there are an awful lot of shoe sales waiting for bargain mavens.

CHAPTER 12

Inferior Merchandise or Top Quality: Which Is It?

"The worst thing bargain hunters can do is to lower their standards just to keep prices down. You can get those bargains *and* maintain your style and integrity at the same time. If you end up without quality or what you like, with something that isn't you, you're not doing it effectively. My whole reason for bargain shopping is because I want the *best*, the very best. I know what I want. I know what I need. And I get it precisely because I know where to get the best bargains, the true bargains, which are top quality, inside and out."

—Josette Serlin,
Fashion Bargain Columnist

It doesn't always follow that expensive clothes are well made—or that inexpensive clothes are poorly made.

Many top designers are going abroad to manufacture apparel not because foreign factories provide superior workmanship—some do, others haven't the training and sophistication yet—but because it costs less. Many designer/ manufacturers are so busy being successful that they haven't the time to spend in the Far East monitoring the workmanship of their products, and that can mean trouble.

Additionally, while designers can't be faulted for pursuing new fashion horizons by experimenting with new color processes and fabrications, they will not always use materials with the standards of quality and practicality that consumers now demand, or test them thoroughly enough. On America's sale racks smart shoppers with an eye for a bargain will always find examples of these questionable experiments along with merchandise of impeccable style and execution. The other day I slipped on an oversized shirt dress which was, on first observation, a real bargain find reduced from $69 to 50 percent off the last sale price—grand total, $15. Women in the communal dressing room ooh-ed and aah-ed when I put it on. On closer investigation of the material I found that what I had first thought was uncut silk, cotton and a small polyester content was in fact 100 percent rayon. That's fine for a blouse, but for a dress of heavy texture it would have brought on some very heated days in the business world. I left that literally breath-less "bargain" to somebody else.

On the other hand, I was recently browsing in a discount department store where I discovered a black-and-white 100 percent cotton knit top, distinguished not only by a true fit but by delicately executed workmanship at the collar. Cost: $10. In a pricier place, it could have been $30 or more. Cool, versatile, all-season, it was a "real" bargain, where as the shirtdress was not.

It's a mistake to assume designers know better, that whatever innovation they've introduced is worthy of the price they put on it and our automatic admiration. I'm personally convinced that quality *does* come at every price level, although it's far more important to scrutinize an expensive garment than it is a faddish fun item which, at $5, will pay for itself after a few wearings. But whether it's priced at a bargain-lover's $10 or at $100, what you buy should meet some basic standards of quality. To be an effective bargain hunter it's not enough to be able to spot sale signs and compute price reductions. Learning to recognize quality is vital. Here are the most important things to look for when you're on the bargain trail. As I've said before, low price alone does not constitute a bargain.

Is it first quality? A top designer label doesn't promise you a well-made garment. You've got to look inside, at the seams and hems, the stitching, buttons, and fabric. (Photo by Ebet Roberts)

FABRIC—It's just not enough to say, "I like it." After you take it home, you'll change your mind if the material

- itches
- pills
- releases or retains body heat
- bags
- shrinks
- fades
- creases
- must be dry cleaned
- quickly loses its weight or luster

The composition of the fabric makes all the difference. The first place to look, if a garment strikes your fancy, is at the label describing fabric content and instructions about care. Consider the climate in which you live, the sometimes cryptic care instructions that advise you that the manufacturer takes no responsibility for maintenance of the garment, as well as where and how often you'll be wearing the garment.

Where it used to be relatively easy to weigh the virtues of 100 percent cotton, wool, silk and linen—for centuries, the principal fabrics for clothing—we're now faced with "blends." These include all-natural blends like mohair and wool, or cotton and silk; all-synthetic blends like rayon, spandex and nylon; and a combination of the two: silk, cotton and rayon.

Sometimes there's no way to tell whether after the first washing your garment will retain all the qualities that made it appealing to you when you bought it. But it's safe to say that although synthetics have come a long way in their ability to ape fabrics from natural sources, 100 percent synthetics simply do not always wear as well, feel as good or retain their original beauty. On the other hand, blends that mix natural with synthetic are often excellent in both upkeep and wearability.

The fabric should, at the least, pass a simple visual/tactile test. If it is flimsy or mottled, scratchy and brittle, if the color's washed out or unnaturally bright, then you've got trouble. Try it on. Don't necessarily expect these negatives to be corrected after a washing or dry cleaning. When a garment is new, the fabric is presented to you as beautifully as the manufacturer could make it. If it's not appealing now, it probably never will be—and that's no bargain.

Neither is a garment a bargain when, just hanging in the store, the fabric is already drooping, puckering and pulling. That means it has not been cut on the grain, and in all probability the use of a steam iron won't make it fall any more gracefully.

COLOR—Today, many garments are piece-dyed. The color is added *after* the cloth has been woven, rather than to the individual strands of yarn. This trend is most obvious in shirts. Look on the inside and if you see only the shadow of color or design from the outside, you know it has been piece-dyed. That means this surface coloring is more vulnerable to being washed out. Most consumers believe "color fast" clothing is the norm. Yet with dependency on factories in India and other nations, along with the advent of fabric blends where the color might be retained by one element of the blend better than the other, true color fast is actually a sometime thing. If you go ahead and buy, consider washing by hand for the first few times a new garment with deep, brilliant colors or a print which looks as if certain colors may fade.

STITCHING—There's a downhill trend in stitching as manufacturers attempt to save on the cost of thread. Seams are flimsier than ever before because sometimes up to half the usual number of stitches per inch are used. Look inside the garment, especially at the pressure points—crotch, seat, underarms, collar. If the seams are loose, corners have been cut.

Finished safety stitching inside a garment is imperative. Otherwise, you'll have non-stop unraveling which will eventually cause a permanent hole in the garment. An open, finished and pressed inner seam lasts longer and feels better than a rough safety stitch which sticks up like a cowlick. Covered open and pressed seams are a mark of quality in better trousers.

And don't forget to check the symmetry of seams at the shoulders and under the arms on a print shirt, and on skirts and slacks, too. If they don't match or if they hang so the left side of you looks worse than the right, you're looking at slopping sewing techniques.

POCKETS—Check to see if the backtacking, the extra seam at the pocket corners, is secure. Although jeans can have unlined pockets, dress pants pockets should be lined, preferably with sateen or a strong cotton. Tricot and gauze linings tend to rip and lose their shape. Pocket linings should also be stitched twice to prevent unraveling, then bar tacked at the bottom and top of the pocket opening. If the fabric on the outside of the pocket has been cut skimpily, the inside will likely gap and pop out, which looks terrible.

ZIPPERS—Unless actually used purely for ornamentation, zippers should not be visible. On a garment you'll be washing many times, make sure the zipper (or snaps) won't stain the fabric with rust. Any rusty discoloration *before* you buy is a telltale sign. Also, the way a zipper fastens at the base is particularly important on jackets, since you'll be pulling it up and down for at least one season, hopefully more. Shoddy stitching and finishing will be a problem. I've found that children's jackets are sometimes made with the shoddiest zippers of all, when they should actually be the strongest. You'll have lots of tears if your young one can't zip it up himself because the seams are ripping or catching in the zipper when it's used, and the zipper itself is either too fine or fails to work half the time. If you have to play Houdini in the store to extricate yourself from the garment, don't buy it.

WAISTS AND HEMS—Make sure that on the outside the cuff or waistband and the body of the item have been cut on the same bias or slant. Failure to do so will make the two separate pieces look like different materials. Elastic waistbands should be covered or hidden—those sewn directly inside the waistband are cheaper to manufacture. The waistband on men's dress pants should have what is known as a "second sleeve," an inner lining which helps the garment retain shape. The waistband should be designed on a slight curve that enhances the fit of the garment.

Women's plaid or stripped skirts and dresses can't be hemmed any which way: Hems should fold without cutting across a pattern. That means the garment must be properly designed from the very top. Although occasionally denim skirt seams are visible on the outside, most other hems should be invisible and uniformly level all around. A dip in the back or puckers in the front indicate the hem has been incorrectly stitched or the material has stretched. Hems for easily unraveled fabrics such as rayon or silk should be finished with extra care.

COLLARS—Except when style dictates, a collar should not be stiff, but soft and malleable. Better dress shirts and blouses should be sewn with interfacing—an extra piece of material inside that will prolong its life. Watch the collar stitching. Too tight and the collar may pucker in the wash; any skipped stitches in the collar and it may mean eventual unraveling, something particularly difficult to correct without costly professional tailoring.

BUTTONS—Another cost-cutting element for a manufacturer is the use of polyester-based buttons rather than the more durable, more attractive pearlized variety. But if the garment as a whole shows promise, a side trip to a button specialty store can restore the value of your purchase. Button holes, too, must be inspected. If they have not been properly finished, unraveling can undermine the overall look and life of the garment.

TRIMMING AND ORNAMENTATION—If button holes, seams, pockets, and collars have bits of thread sticking out, the garment hasn't been properly trimmed. Can you do it without harming the material? Has the ornamentation—decals, costume jewelry—been designed to survive a visit to the dry cleaner or wash? I've seen many sweaters on sale racks that have been attractively designed—but not for repeated use by real people. The "special effects" have begun to unravel after just a few try-ons.

LININGS—It's almost impossible to find a jacket or coat these days that has an elegant satin lining. So often, linings are an afterthought or a manufacturer's cost-saver, even in higher-priced goods. They hang in there, limp and misshapen. Some-times you can't get your hand into a sleeve because of the bunched-up material inside. Linings should be tailored a bit smaller than the garment. Too big and they assume an annoying life of their own, hanging outside the garment, or creating little bulges inside. Smaller-than-needed linings, on the other hand, pull a garment from its natural shape, creating unsightly creases and eventual tearing that is difficult to repair. Also, remember to *feel* the lining. If it's tacky to the touch, pass it up. If there's no lining at all, be sure that the jacket hangs properly on its own. Otherwise, the lapel may flap about and the garment feel uncomfortable.

CUFFS—Quality "single-needle" stitching, often advertised in better shirts and blouses, is more attractive to the eye and longer-lasting. Double-needle stitching tends to pucker. Check to make certain, especially on synthetics, that a finished inside seam will protect the garment from fraying.

SWEATERS—That phrase "full-fashion" is an indication of quality. Sweaters labeled as such are knit rather than cut to pattern, so that the edges are finished, with the seams knitted, not sewn. That means when the sweater's washed it won't lose its shape or suffer possible unraveling of seams. The knits for cheaply-made sweaters are stretched and cut for maximum yardage and, after washing, may shrivel up.

OUTERWEAR—With the popularity of down as filling for winter coats and vests, consumers have had to attempt to weigh the virtues of feathers they can't see. Federal standards require that the product be labeled "down-filled" or "down" only if it contains no less than 80 percent down, plus waterfowl feathers totaling *no more* than 18 percent. Otherwise, the product must be called a "blend," and the exact ratio of the combination must be on the label. Feather linings, whatever the mix, are warm, but waterfowl feathers are coarser, which means the garment's outer fabric must meet the test. Unless the fabric weave is tight and has a so-called high thread count, the feathers—and this sometimes happens with certain man-made linings—will begin poking through. The best bet for inside is what the government calls "light, fluffy filaments growing out of one quill point but without any quill shaft." Also, if the feathers feel as if they're in clumps, the jacket is a poor investment.

FURS—The best furs are such high ticket items that the *bargain chic* maven must pay special attention to quality. Seek out reputable fur retailers, preferably those solely in the business of selling furs, rather than stores that sell them without specialists to help you. Many furs on the lower end of the price spectrum are expected to shed; in some cases, a thorough cleaning will help. Furs bought in resale must be checked to make sure the hides have not dried out or cracked, or the fur itself isn't coming out in unsightly tufts. Also, make sure the lining in the coat is heavy enough and adequately reinforced to withstand the weight of the fur. Fur alterations are costly, so ask as many questions up front as possible!

Applying these stringent tests to clothing is a time-consuming process. Sometimes you'll be so infatuated with a garment that it won't matter if the manufacturing is a touch suspect. This probably won't be an addition to your "timeless" bargain chic wardrobe but it will be fun to wear, however long it lasts. Forcing quality control standards on your wardrobe is important for those clothes that *will* constitute a timeless look. And remember that unless every designer on the fasion spectrum spent time in Timbuktu overseeing manufacture of his latest line, the chances that merchandise will be a little less than perfectly made are very good. So don't let only the price of a garment convince you that it's above reproach. *Bargain chic* principles must be applied.

You should be prepared now to shop for quality at the same time you are looking for bargains. The soundest words on the subject of quality and value were put to me thusly:

"The better I've become at bargain hunting, the fewer clothes I own and the more I have to wear. What I own is well planned out," says Annette Swanberg, co-author of Los Angeles-area bargain resource guides and fashion books. "I own less, in part, because it really takes a fantastic bargain to excite me—a diamond in the rough. Those of us who know how to find them are jaded. We see so *many* bargains they have to be superb in quality and value to really catch our attention."

CHAPTER 13

Men and Shopping

"The best bargain is buying nothing."
—Allen K., 32, art dealer

"For the longest time, I avoided bargains because I had no concept of what they were, other than a good price on something. But what *was* a good price? It meant nothing because I never went shopping—I *hated* shopping—and my wardrobe reflected it. If a sales person said something was a good deal, I believed it. When I actually went into stores I got intimidated real fast. There were so many things to buy. Where should I start? Everything looked good. I didn't notice anything on sale, because I never really looked.

"Now I go into a store and the first thing I ask is if anything is on sale; in fact, the salespeople almost always have something good to tell you about that is a bargain. I haven't gone all the way over to the other side as far as bargains go. It's a question of finding something I like. If it's on sale, I buy it. I think if you're real careful about *how* you shop you can definitely stay in style for less. The amazing thing for me is to talk about style at all. Until a couple of years ago I couldn't have cared less about clothes. Now I'm really conscientious. I dress to stand out, to make a statement about *me*. I'm not the richest guy around and learning about sales has really made a difference. I never thought I'd be saying such a thing."
—Jeff B., 28, musician

Highly trained female bargain shoppers enter a store in a combat stance—noses thrust forward, brows wrinkled, jaws set, pocketbooks clenched. They listen. They look. It's a jungle in there, and these soldiers of fortune have no intention of being eaten alive. They're tuned into the environment, they expect surprises and welcome them as tests of their courage and commitment to the cause.

Their view of shopping is diametrically opposed to the male shopper's traditional "Wait on me—that's what I'm paying for" sensibility. Historically, there probably have been as few men who actually enjoyed shopping as those who could spot a great fashion bargain.

"So many women are professional bargain hunters," says Leonard Atkin, president of NBO (National Brands Outlet) men's off-price clothing stores. "Men feel it demeans them to bargain hunt. They're preconditioned to doubt a bargain, skeptical and suspicious of the truth of it. Part of this skepticism has been their *own* inability to make a decision about what to buy. They're creatures of habit fashion-wise; much more so than women. For men, shopping has never been a hobby. It's a duty they discharge reluctantly."

Are men *really* as negative about shopping as they're cracked up to be—and why? I sought out some typical American males in various walks of life, and asked them about shopping and bargains.

"If I don't know what I'm shoping for I don't like it—it's a drag," said a 45-year-old teacher who gravitates toward wash-and-wear shirts and polyester pants because they're "easy to maintain. They don't look 'great'—I know that—but they never look creased or sloppy. What I hate most of all is going shopping with someone else who ignores me the whole time, acts like I don't exist."

"I do not go shopping with anybody except my wife," a 40-year-old suited-up college professor told me. "In fact, I prefer to defer to her. I rarely make major purchases without her. I am not a sophisticated-enough shopper to rely on my own judgment of quality. She get's much better bargains than I do, but I don't have the time to find them. Anyway, discount stores are so confusing to shop in; it's hard to find the stuff there. And if I did buy anything, would it fall apart when it's dry cleaned?"

A 25-year-old administrative assistant: "I never go shopping unless I need something. Somebody will tell me about a sale, but if I don't need anything, I won't go. I guess I don't really like shopping very much. The funny thing is, sometimes a week or two after I hear about a sale, I realize I *do* need exactly what they offered. If I had thought about it earlier, I could have taken advantage of it. Maybe I'm stubborn. But I just don't like crowds, and the pressure to buy once I'm there."

The men quoted above voice characteristic wariness of shopping. They feel passive when they visit stores, and figure that it's probably easier to let somebody else do the picking and chosing. Keep in mind what one man said—that he hates feeling insignificant when he shops with somebody else. Another admired his wife's ability to sale shop, but imagined that if he looked for sales he'd get lost and confused—and the merchandise wouldn't hold up anyway. And while admitting he often misjudged his wardrobe needs, the third man stayed away from sales because of the crowds and the pressure to purchase.

As a result of this historical dislike of shopping in general and buying a bargain along the way, American men have developed an international reputation for being notably unfashionable. This "why bother?" mentality undoubtedly influenced menswear designers, who hestitated to rock the boat and instead supplied the same old styles and fabrics and colors to generations of American men.

But men's attitudes towards shopping and fashion are beginning to change. In his recent book, *Dressing Right*, Charles Hix noted that, while men generally continue to be embarrassed to admit caring about how they look, the time has come, in Hix's opinion, to "junk that thinking," to eradicate the myth that women know how to dress men better than men dress themselves. He feels it is time for men to heed designer Bill Blass's notion that "women are no more sure of their taste than men."

"The first step in dressing right is to recognize that clothing is an extension of yourself, not a conspiracy with a loss of self as the ultimate goal," Hix wrote in his exhortation to men to take pride in their wardrobes.

My conversations with sympathetic retailers and fashion experts indicate the presence of a new man on the scene who *is* concerned about his appearance. To prove it, he's shopping more, and with greater independence. Leonard McGill, author of *Stylewise: A Man's Guide to Looking Good for Less*, judges that there are now millions of bona fide male fashion mavens roaming about, determined to look good and, according to industry statistics, willing to spend from $500 to $800 a year to achieve it; and this is true even if "shopping for clothes is still suspect in many men's minds. They don't have a problem browsing in the sporting goods or hardware departments, but clothing scares them."

McGill's "new breed" even goes to stores *by himself*— sometimes. More often he still tends to take along a friend or spouse. However, even harder than overcoming the "shopping-is-women's-work" mentality is the manly suspicion of anything resembling a bargain.

"Even if they are secretly big bargain hunters, as I am," McGill says over his shoulder as I follow him around an off-price men's store where he's determined to find a pair of Fila shorts at less than half price (he has a salesman looking in the stockroom and rifling through drawers), "they usually don't feel comfortable admitting it."

The negative male perspective on bargains seems to go along with a man's relatively inflexible view of quality. If it's well-made, it *should* cost more, men generally believe. While women have at one time or another usually hemmed a skirt or sewn on a button, perhaps made an entire dress, men's views on quality are based on untested and outdated theories.

- A 38-year-old dyed-in-the-wool anti-bargain male executive argues: "If the buttons look miserable, I don't even bother looking at the rest of the garment because it's probably cheap too."
- A 35-year-old lawyer: "I remember those perma-press shirts I wore as a kid. They always looked terrible, and I wore them anyway and acted like I didn't care about clothes. Now I won't buy anything that has any synthetic material in it at all. I just won't. I'll always go for the 100 percent wool suits, even if they're twice as expensive as a blend and you can't tell the difference."
- A 19-year-old-male college student: "Clothes without name brands have to be junky. It means the manufacturer is trying to hide something."
- And a 50-year-old broker: "You have to *pay* for a designer name. The places that claim to sell real designer stuff at lower prices must be faking. How is it possible to be able to find the same stuff that much cheaper? It's got to be a rip off, so I never buy it."

A recent fashion industry study of the shopping behavior and taste of 1000 men living in Miami, Chicago, Atlanta, Kansas City, New York, Dallas, Phoenix, San Francisco, Los Angeles and Chicago found that, on the average, men buy clothes on sale only 25 percent of the time. Those in the most sophisticated and socially aware segment of America's male population, called "The Updated Man" in the survey, say they don't really think about prices— "If I like something, I buy it." And they have a typical aversion to the phrase "factory outlet."

"Buying clothes is my main extravagance," say these trendsetters, many of whom are unaware that the definition of the terms "factory outlet" and "discount" have evolved to conform to their own self-image as men who are:

- smart and sophisticated
- aware of current fashion trends
- distinctive in fashion style
- masculine-looking
- sexy-looking

The plain fact is that the Updated Man can find trendy, fashionable, distinctive, masculine, sexy, smart and sophisticated clothing at bargain prices virtually all over the USA. This apparel will conform to the American man's traditional desire for

- high quality materials
- durable, low-wrinkle fabrics
- quality manufacturing
- comfort

How does an Updated Man, or one who aspires to be, find these gems without sweating it out or making a fool of himself?

He loosens up traditional preconceptions of shopping, and begins to realize that however liberated he is from more conservative males who care little for style, sophistication and image in clothing, he may unwittingly remain the passive shopper that higher-priced, more traditional men's stores cultivate, stores like the one that placed this psychologically compelling newspaper advertisement recently:

> "You're on a very tight schedule. You arrive at your
> men's store at the appointed time. A salesman is
> waiting with a selection of suits from the makers
> you prefer in the price range you favor. A custom

tailor is on hand to fit you and alterations are free.
While all this may sound too good, let us assure
you it's true and happens every day...."

Service of this caliber can be seductive; it also encourages a
man to sit back and let other people shop for him—and spend
his hard-earned money. It would be very suprising if such a
store brought out any sale items for his perusal. The man who
expresses his dislike for pressured shopping will be, in this
situation, under enormous pressure to spend large sums of
money.

But he needn't go this route. He can find the happy
medium in the wide variety of store types discussed here.
Some provide little service. Others offer more, but only upon
request. And just because a store promises bargains does not
mean the absence of sales help and tailoring on the premises.

Men who haven't checked out these new fashion forums are
missing not only some of the best values in contemporary
clothes, but some of the most forward fashions as well as
classics. And not all of these so-called "off-price" or "factory
outlet" centers expect you to shop alone and trust your own
intuition and fashion knowledge.

Remember that each store or chain is positioned to appeal
to customers in a slightly different way from competitors.
Menswear centers offering "best buys" run the gamut from
plush environments that look much like department stores
with about the same proportion of merchandise to floor
space, to the airplane hangar alternatives, where clothing—
lots and lots of it—stretches everywhere the eye can see, with
very little attempt at elegant presentation.

While the hangar-like stores seem to say that money saved
on atmosphere by the owners will be savings passed onto
customers, you won't know whether this is true or not until
you look through the apparel.

No matter what the "look" of the store itself, the "look" of
the clothing is more important.

Stan was surprised to find salespeople to help him in a large men's off-price store. But the real surprise came when he found the same brands he was used to seeing in Bloomingdale's. When I left him he was trying on sports jackets. . . . I think he may still be there. (Photo by Ebet Roberts)

- Is it fresh-looking, well-protected, well-labeled? If not, this is probably not the first stop this clothing has made, nor is it totally up-to-date.
- Are you so overwhelmed with the sheer onslaught of merchandise that you can't begin to figure out what you want, and soon forget what you need? Bring a list along with you. Ask questions.
- Is the checkout system convenient? If you are on a tight schedule, make sure it doesn't take more time than you have to pay for your bargain.
- If you are the type of person who likes some degree of service—somebody to make sure the sport coat hangs flat across the shoulders, for example—is it available?

"Everybody knows women are wise shoppers," runs a current Wool Council radio advertisement. But given the chance, men can be, too. "The fact is," says Leonard Atkin of NBO menswear, "women today have less time to go shopping for and with men, so men are learning to do it themselves."

The best ways to learn are to observe—and to ask questions. Here's what to ask when you're visiting your favorite traditional department store or specialty men's shop:

- Does the store plan any sales soon?
- When sales commence, what is the usual initial markdown—20 percent, 25 percent higher? How long does it take for second, third and/or final markdowns to appear?
- Where are the sales racks—in the men's department proper, or on another floor? (Some stores take everything to a "Sale Area.")
- Does the store feature any private labels and, if so, are they on sale or expected to be reduced? (Sometimes you can get a knowledgeable salesperson to let you know whether the source of a private label is the same as a famous designer line.)

- Does the store have a return/exchange/money-back policy on markdowns?
- Can sale items be altered by the store?
- Are there any window samples that are available for markdown prices? (Sure, you'll wait while the salesperson asks the department manager!)

"The truth is that most men do care, and care deeply, what they look like and what other people think of their appearance," says veteran retailer Mortimer Levitt of the Custom Shop chain of men's shops. "You know how good you feel when you buy a new suit, shirt, or tie that you believe is exactly right for you.

"When you look attractive, you feel attractive, and with a little know-how," Levitt believes, "you can have that good feeling...all the time."

And, the *bargain chic* way, save money too.

CHAPTER 14

Kids' Clothes

"Mommy, is it on sale?"

As the mother of two young children, I'm constantly faced with clothing price tags rivaling those of adult apparel. How can it be? Kids are smaller. It simply doesn't take as much fabric to sew a three-year-old's jogging suit as it does a grown man's.

Since children's clothing is more fashion-forward than ever before, it costs more than ever before. Designers don't mind designing for pipsqueaks either, not as long as their parents want them to dress like adults.

Parents with pre-teens and teens tell me it gets much worse—$70 for a pair of jeans to make their child feel "accepted" in school. What's a person to do?

By following the general guidelines in other chapters of this book, parents can locate heavily discounted clothing for children—in department stores, outlets, and in the exploding off-price children's area, as well as, very, very inexpensively, in second-hand stores and at garage sales.

If a parent plays the "looking ahead to next season" game, a child's wardrobe that is trendy yet practical and age-appropriate *can* be constructed on a shoestring. All you need other than foresight is extra closet space.

First, let's talk about the special demands of kids' clothing that will prove itself every day in the schoolyard.

COLOR—Esoteric colors are harder to match, and therefore are less of a bargain in the long run. My daughter has a pair of screaming lavender pants that were purchased inexpensively, but the shrieks and sighs she emits whenever she tries to find a matching top are less pretty to my ears than the pants are to my eyes. Constructing a kidswear color profile of denims, basic reds, blues, wines, yellows, greens will start you in the right direction. Whatever Johnny takes out of the drawer will match automatically.

COTTON OR POLY—Each has virtues. I prefer cotton because in the summer it breathes so well and, when stains appear, you can treat them without wondering whether the fibers will disintegrate or the fabric stretch, as polys often do. Polys, too, are notorious stain catchers, and even the newest fibers tend to pill and lose shape. But they're sometimes tougher-made and comfortingly warm in cold weather. And they are often available more cheaply. Watch out for iron-on decals applied to kids' actionwear as decoration. It tends to peel off in the washer and dryer and is not easily reapplied. Last time I tried, the decal shriveled up and died, leaving a permanent gluey smudge on the sweatshirt, and an unhappy child!

MORE ON FABRICS—Kids' clothes are going to be in the washer as much as they'll be on the kids, so the fabric must be up to it. For both my son's and daughter's pants in winter I gravitate to denim and curduroy, two toughies that last and last. Often I iron patches *inside* the knees to protect that vulnerable area. Beware when you buy corduroy, however, of an overly fuzzy nap (it's a sign of cheapness) and a stiff feel which can mean too much sizing has been applied to give the impression of a weightier fabric. Once the chemicals wash out, the pants may look forlornly thin and be uncomfortable to wear, or cardboard-like and full of wrinkles.

You can find many good buys on flannels in the winter, but be sure you know the difference between the less expensive, printed variety, which has the pattern applied to the front of the fabric, and the more expensive flannels, which tend to keep their luster longer and are woven with pre-dyed yarn.

WORKMANSHIP—You need security in the seat and crotch area of slacks, and under the arms and around button holes and collar of shirts and blouses. Look for seams that are finished and reinforced. Otherwise, you'll be in for the annoyance of unraveling. Today's apparel is often sewn with fewer stitches per inch than used to be acceptable. That means r-i-p-s galore. Feeble-looking stitching probably means trouble.

Where the Bargains Are

Don't wait for "back to school specials" to dress your kids well. Here's my rundown of where and how to apply *bargain chic* to the little ones.

Department Stores—Department stores are reducing kiddie wear an average of 25 to 30 percent *throughout the year and in season* on select "sale" days. It's not unlikely that you can purchase a winter jacket for a child in August or September at reductions that rival spring sales, and the selection is much better.

I really stock up at season's end when designer children's clothing is sold *at cost or below,* amazing as that may seem. You won't find the assortment late in the season, but you will find the quality—one big plus in shopping for kids in department stores.

Off-Price—Several national chains, such as Kids 'R' Us," Marshalls, Burlington Coat Factory, J. Brannum and the Children's Outlet, now offer 33 to 50 percent off kids' clothing every day of the year. With this policy in effect you won't have to mesh your busy schedule with a department store's occasional bargain-binge days. But don't expect most of the apparel in all off-price stores to be outrageously reduced. Instead, it runs the gamut from the polite bargains of Kids 'R' Us and the Children's Outlet to lucky streaks at places like Marshalls and Burlington, where, if you find a rack with additional markdowns, you can make a killing.

Discount Stores—K-Mart, Caldor, Gold Circle, and Venture are among the best places to find a wide selection of fashion forward *and* traditional kids' clothing. Discount stores stage frequent markdowns. But to win here, you've got to be a shopper who is able to discern between the inexpensively made outfits and those that will last. Stay away from 100 percent poly anything in discount stores. It's miserable, for some reason, particularly in pajamas. It creases and retains every stain under the sun, and will cause your children to become overheated.

Discount stores are havens of rugged, mid-priced kids' sneakers, summer sandals and slippers, as well as underwear and surprisingly nice outerwear. Learn when "spot sales" occur. Many discount stores have them, and you can really stock up when everything on the sale rack becomes $1 for an hour.

Speaking of stocking up, bulk buying is the way to go to save money on children's wear. Unlike most adults, who want a variety of clothes for work and leisure and are judged—perhaps too severely at times—by their ability to "look different" every day, kids don't require quite that degree of variety. They need the basics—jeans, tops, sneakers, sweaters, jogging suits, skirts and a couple of frillier dresses for girls. That's the kind of wardrobe that calls out for bulk buying. Last year I came across a rack of jeans, all brand name, some "designer" quality, in a Kids 'R' Us, and no matter what the original price, there they all were for $5.99. I walked out with eight pairs—four for each kid, in escalating sizes. It was $50 well spent. And, unless your child is difficult to fit, in smaller sizes boys and girls slack and tops can be worn by either sex.

Second Hand—A garage full of kids' clothes. That's what I had to choose from at one recent spring sale. The woman had saved everything her kids ever wore. The T-shirts were classic. So were the little girls' dresses with adorable, hand-wrought smocking. At second-hand events, I always go straight for the hand-knit sweaters and boys' blue blazers. Last time out, I found a blazer in fine condition with a Brooks Brothers label for my son, priced at $1.50. After a quick trip to the cleaners, it looked like a million. Check out local church and synogogue bazaars too, where the clothing is usually high quality and very inexpensive. I prefer these sales to the "resale" stores for kids'

The best stores really milk you for kids' jogging clothes, but you'll find respectable copies of Grasshopper and other high-end brands in discount department stores and lower-end children's wear centers. (Photo by Ebet Roberts)

clothing, which tend to make markdowns of 50 percent from the *original* price of the merchandise, even when it's faded and out of style. You can do as well in most retail stores today with *fresh* merchandise.

Remember that young children grow so fast that a second-hand item bought at a garage sale is likely to have been worn very little. If you look for those relatively new items you can provide your child with an amazingly contemporary wardrobe very inexpensively, especially on outerwear, sweaters and dressy clothing—apparel that if purchased new would be high-end stuff!

New Best Buys for Kids—They come from Mainland China and are virtually all 100 percent cotton or $^{65}/_{35}$ cotton/poly weaves that are surprisingly strong and appealing. Work-manship is of old-fashioned top quality. Look carefully on labels to find the source of your kids' clothing. Many top designers are beginning to use Far Eastern factories. The cost to them is lower, and so it should be to you. Brands like Popsicle, Happy Kids and Hush Puppies, to name a few demonstrating quality in workmanship and materials, have been using Chinese manufac-turing expertise for some time and offer a characteristic com-bination of basic kids' clothes and those with a fashion-forward touch. Other brands seem to utilize patterns that have probably been sitting in China's factories since before the Revolution, so the styles are considerably more traditional. You'll most likely find such clothing at urban and suburban discount department stores.

Costumes: My kids love to dress up and put on "shows." All they need to start up the imagination is the right garb. I've come up with a few silly old things of my own, but hard-pressed for variety, I found an amazing array of brand-new, sufficiently gaudy clothing to fuel their fantasies. When the Michael Jackson craze abated, shirts and jackets with glitter and tassles and other ornamentation were reduced to a dollar or two. Prowl in the deepest discount, second-hand and "odd lot and schlock" type stores for clothing that may look way out of fashion to you, but has the right mystique to inspire kids' fantasies. "Mod" clothes from the sixties with bold flowers, wild collars and platform shoes are ideal. The last time I took my kids to the Volunteers of America, they went wild dressing up. And my daughter's "Cabbagy" baby doll went home with a complete and very beautiful wardrobe of size 1 dresses at a quarter each.

Kids' Shoes: Many generations have been brought up to believe that the harder the sole the better the shoe for small children. But podiatrists now suggest that crepe or rubber-soled shoes help cushion impact on those tiny feet and bodies. And, of course, once you break away from the notion that your kids don't need straight-jackets on their feet, bargain options are wide open. Check regularly with discount department stores and bargain stores that tend to buy out perfectly good sneaker models ornamented with slightly un-chic messages. For a while there in the late 1970s many of the kids in my neighborhood were happy enough to romp in "Bicentennial 1776-1976" sneakers, and my children recently had no trouble wearing 1984 Summer Olympics models.

Warning: You'll sometimes come across kids' shoes of man-made materials that at first glance cleverly ape leather but they wear and breathe poorly and therefore are no bargain, except as "special occasion" shoes.

With so much quality apparel to be plucked for children, you simply don't have to buy junk. But, on the other hand, beware of "designer" kids' clothes. While some designers, including Calvin Klein, Ralph Lauren and Ruth Scharf, make apparel expressly for children, others are now licensing their names to be applied to clothes for little ones made by outsiders. While sometimes the result is top quality, don't let that famous name label turn your head. Apply even *more* stringent standards of quality than you would for yourself, because kids wear clothes harder.

Lastly, let me address the issue of what kids like. We

Nicholas and Allegra love to dress up and put on shows. I found them these Michael Jackson-type glitter tops reduced to $1 each. (Photo by Ebet Roberts)

bargain hunters sometimes go overboard. Enthusiasm leads to questionable purchases. But when buying for someone else, a child included, it's no bargain if its ugly, uncomfortable, lacks style and is cheap-looking. My kids already know what "on sale" means. If it's not, I probably won't buy it—with exceptions for classics like saddle shoes and down jackets. While they're aware of our family budget they also know *what they like*. Forcing any child to wear a miserable garment bought solely for its sale value is a mistake, and it may lead to difficulty later on. They might, for example, go on a permanent sale strike and you'll have to shell out for those $70 jeans whether you like it or not.

CHAPTER 15

Shopping and Guilt: Feeling Good About Spending Less

Some years ago an article I wrote on bargain shopping for a major publication was rejected because the editors believed the people I interviewed were too healthy and normal. They included a stockbroker who dispensed free bargain tips and resources between high-stakes financial calls, a novelist whose perennial lack of funds influenced her bargain-smart decisions, a young executive whose hobby had become "beating the system" by buying his clothing always under wholesale, and a young mother who upon the birth of her child had reapportioned a fixed clothing budget to fit three by going after bargains.

The wise consumerism and the enjoyment they found in their individual quests for *bargain chic* simply didn't wash with these editors who refused to believe me. Their theory was, "Bargain shopping is a neurosis. The people who do it must be sick."

Times have changed. Just the other day, I noticed a gigantic sign plastered across the window of a fine boutique: "HUGE BARGAINS." And this elegant store wasn't even going out of business! The busloads of consumers who pour into factory outlet shopping centers look forward to two things—saving money and having a ball. Nobody would dare tell them to have their heads examined.

"Beating the system is a thrill for a shopper," says Dr. Herbert Freudenberger, a New York psychiatrist who authored *Situational Anxieties* and *Burn-Out.* "The shopper feels euphoric: 'I didn't comply with the rules . . . I *outdid* all of them—the manufacturer, the store, shoppers who aren't as smart!' Bargain shopping is legitimate; it's a chance for people to make a statement about the system—and to survive within it, too."

I'll call him Bill. One day on the park bench, during a conversation about shopping, Bill became overheated. You see, Bill hates bargains.

"They never look right," he said with the assurance of somebody who's never bought one or once had too many foisted upon him. "They're soiled or ripped or cheap. I would feel as if I had second best if I bought something on sale. Besides, I have very specific tastes. Bargains are for people who don't care about how they look. I wish I didn't have to spend as much as I do on my clothing, but if you want to stand out and make an impression you have to pay for it."

Bill is one of those people who simply *can't* buy a bargain. "They wouldn't be caught dead going after one, because they're much too image conscious," Dr. Freudenberger contends. "As children, they might have been forced to wear hand-me-downs that made them look terrible; their parents bought clothing that was cheap and fell apart. Maybe other kids laughed at them. These people have such anger and resentment that they *must* buy whatever's most expensive, even if they don't feel comfortable with their expensive image, or can't afford it."

For every Bargain Hater there is a Bargain-a-holic who compulsively stocks bargains by the bushel but inevitably disregards both the tenets of *bargain chic* and the family budget.

While the great mass of smart shoppers in the middle reap psychic and economic profit from the discovery of a "good buy," bargain-a-holics become mired in a destructive shopping syndrome.

Bargain-a-holics buy on impulse. Afraid to pass up a good deal, driven not just to beat the system but to buy better and more bargains than anybody else, their approach to sale shopping is, according to Dr. Edward Christophersen, a psychologist at the University of Kansas Medical School, "like the gambler who's been burned three times but figures he'll surely win next time. Bargain-a-holics never understand the odds against making a wise purchase without thinking or researching. Instead, all they have is the urgency to get it more cheapily than anybody else."

One of the more poignant shoppers' stories I heard came after I'd interviewed a famous movie actor who happened to tell me proudly that his wife was a superb bargain hunter. When I phoned her, the celebrity's wife confided to me that she was a bargain hunter who wished she wasn't. "But it's gotten out of hand," she told me. "My husband makes tons of money. I have my own career and do very well. But I still can't get over needing to pay as little as possible for anything I buy. Otherwise, I feel awful. I could afford to buy anything I wanted. But I torture myself over a few dollars. Will it be further reduced? If it's really cheap, I always want more than one. After all, if it's such a good buy, I ought to take two. Then I come home with more than I will ever need. If I don't grab it up, later on I can't stop thinking that I missed out on something."

Bargain-a-holics, says Dr. Christophersen, who is an inveterate bargain hunter himself, are on an endless quest for self-respect. Yet the more they buy, the farther they seem to be from obtaining it. They

- Never feel satisfied with what they've bought for very long.
- Can often afford to pay more for something they like much better.
- Only brag about their successful purchases, but keep their many mistakes a secret.
- Can't put a realistic dollar value on a bargain. The cheaper it is, the better it is to the bargain-a-holic.

- Are easily seduced by advertisements promising savings, and salespeople's hot-air pitches. They will *never* challenge the credibility of the so-called "estimated retail value" of an item.
- Rarely buy months ahead of need because they require instant gratification.
- Shop quickly, without bothering to compare prices.
- Will always buy the sale item, even if it's clearly inferior, if only because they would not be able to boast about a product bought at full price.
- Can't decide how much of anything they really need. More is always better for a bargain-a-holic.
- Never develop a "fund of knowledge" about shopping that influences their buying habits.
- Rarely seek advice about a purchase from an educated consumer.
- Store their useless extra purchases like pack rats and are unwilling to give them up or share them.
- Will respond to small-change bargains with fervor, but end up spending more than they should on big-budget items like cars and houses because they're easily swayed by pitchmen and promises.

The sense of mastery smart shoppers rightfully feel when they conclude a successful purchase never lasts long for bargain-a-holics. Just as they deprive themselves of spending money, so too are they likely to suffer from other addictions or self-deprivations.

The majority of people who love to shop for bargains *do* know when to stop. "For most of us who do develop that 'fund of knowledge' about buying," says Dr. Christophersen, "*really* knowing how and when to save money, and not just on little things, can be pleasurable and rewarding. Bargain shopping gives a person the ultimate feeling of mastery if well done. Read and compare newspaper ads. When you're in the store, look around you. Check the prices. Share information. Ask questions. Wait until the price is right. Bargain if you have to and not just in flea markets. Know what everything *should* cost so that when you see it 'on sale,' you know whether it's really a bargain."

Indeed, the healthy bargain hunter considers sale shopping a serious hobby, one that directly affects his or her life and the lives of those close to them. When I was jotting notes for this book, this is how I characterized my own bargain hunting style.

***

Roberta's Story: Why do I go bargain shopping? It's my hobby. I don't care if I need something or not. If I like it and can afford it, I buy it. I *might* need it soon, anyway. I'm talking about things like a pair of slacks, or a blouse, They're so unearthshatteringly insignificant that I can't get guilty about buying them. Sometimes, I really can't afford something, and I still buy it. My job is steady enough so that I know I'll pay it off next month, and if I waited 'til I did have the cash the bargain would be gone. That would be more stupid, I think. The truth is, I almost never buy *anything* that is not on sale. Let me explain how I operate. When it's summer, I start buying for the next summer—basics, mostly, that never go out of fashion. I also buy stuff that's supposedly for the current season, but in fact is out of place— cottons that you actually can wear all winter; sweaters with cotton or silk content that you can wear through the summer. In the winter bargains keep me feeling good. I start buying sandals and sleeveless clothing and it almost seems like it's warm outside. I think a lot about my clothes. It means a tremendous amount to me to look good. Since I can remember, I've always gotten compliments. People say things like, "I love that outfit. *You* can wear that." So many people seem to think they can't wear very much. They're shy, they don't take any chances.

Whatever the stores put out there in a particular season, they stick to it. They might be "first" with fashion—they go in and shell out the most money for the very earliest shipments, but what they're buying is the same, old stuff. It's odd. These people have always been considered the pace-setters. I actually think I am, and I've always done it my way, on a wing and a prayer and with a certain confidence, too.

CHAPTER 16

How They Do It

Four Bargain Hunters Share Their Secrets

Loaded down with duffel bags, we gathered on a warm spring Sunday afternoon with our bargain loot. Each bargain hunter was asked to model a proud outfit that would exemplify the *bargain chic* philosophy—the quest for personal style, fashion timeliness, quality and price. No complete outfit was to have cost more than $100 *on sale*, but in fact, the total cost per outfit was considerably less. Then, each bargain hunter extraordinaire told how he or she came to be counted in the front ranks of *bargain chic*. Never revealed before, here are their secrets!

Deborah: Teacher and Singer

Since I moved away from home I've never had a lot of money. First I was a student, then a teacher; now I'm a graduate student and a teacher and performer part time. I like to buy bargains not only because it means a larger wardrobe—and I'm the kind of person who likes a bulging closet—but because of the challenge. I have lots of friends who buy the same clothing I do, a couple of weeks before I do, and they pay five times as much as I do. And they're always in debt. One of my friends, who makes about $23,000 a year, prides herself on buying what she calls "expensive" clothes. She immediately assumes that anything reduced is cheaply made and out of style. I take the exact opposite view. Anything reduced is a definite possibility. Because I have a variety of clothing needs to fit my various endeavors, I need to have a large wardrobe of casual, business-like and evening apparel. Some people have asked me whether, if I had more money, I'd abandon my bargain policy out of convenience, so I could experience the pleasure of full price. My answer is definitely not. What would that pleasure be? If I buy a bargain, I don't feel so pressured to wear the outfit to death. Often, at whatever price you buy, when you get home, the purchase isn't that pleasing. You could take it back, but sometimes it's inconvenient.

I grew up with a sister ten years older than I who was very stylish in my view. When I grew up, I had to force myself to develop my own fashion consciousness. What looked good on her didn't always look right for me, no matter how hard I tried. She was taller, thinner, different-looking in clothes. Bargains have helped me develop a sense of myself because I could experiment more.

I've lived in the midwest and the east and have traveled extensively in the south. In each area, there are different perceptions of "chic" which, for better or worse, I at least partially observed. So my own view of what style is changed with the territory. As a result, I still feel as if I'm discovering my own true style. But one thing I know about myself is that I have always been willing to take fashion risks. Whatever ultimate "statement" I make tastewise, it will reflect that quality. The unusual dress I'm wearing in this book looked wild and crazy to me on the rack in the store. It was inappropriate for school or teaching, but I thought I could wear it to parties and auditions. When I discovered it fit—*and it was reduced from $110 to $6.99, and was made by a young New York designer*—I took the plunge. The interesting thing is, my hunch paid off—everybody is enamored of this dress. Many people wouldn't have the courage to wear it. But it makes me

DEBORAH'S OUTFIT

Dress	$ 6.99
Original price	$120.00
Medium heels	$ 5.00
Original price	$ 40.00

Deborah: "This unusual dress looked wild and crazy on the rack in the store, but somehow I thought I could wear it. Then, when it fit, and I saw it was reduced from $110 to $6.99, I had to take the plunge. When I discover something really terrific that's almost a steal, I feel on top of the world." (Photo by Ebet Roberts) feel elegant and it's fun to wear. Those two reasons, coupled with its outrageously low price, make it a real find. Just talking about it brings a smile to my face.

My friends call me the consummate bargain hunter. I mean, if they go out and buy an angora sweater, or jeans, or a winter coat and pay full price, I can find it—either the exact thing or something too close for their comfort—for at least half the price. I'll admit to only one problem as a bargain hunter: Sometimes I overdo it. Recently, when I was on a vacation, I came across some denim jackets, marked down from $30 each to $6.99. I couldn't resist.I bought six of them as presents, but had to cross my fingers that people would take them off my hands. I still have one extra with nobody to wear it. That's definitely a bargain boo-boo. At a recent yard sale I bought nine pair of men's khakis, brand new with tags still on them. They were such a good deal. But they didn't fit me or anybody else. I donated them to charity. Mostly, I love my bargains, and when I discover something really terrific that's almost a steal, I feel very self-confident.

Robert: Bookstore Manager and Far East Tour Guide

I'm a pretty busy person, with a full-time job, and tours, and an occasional film editing project on the side. I like to shop but I don't have unlimited time to do it. And I am on the usual stringent clothing budget. My bargain hunting started some years ago when I was looking for classic clothes, which usually are recycled by designers at much higher prices. I am quite sure of my own style. I like American men's classics that are colorful and relaxed yet stylish and contemporary, like tropical prints or the barracuda jacket which was popular in the 50s but still looks good in the 80s. There are a number of excellent American fashion designers basically rehashing those familiar designs for men—Ralph Lauren, Calvin Klein, Perry Ellis. In a word, they're expensive.

So how do I satisfy these expensive tastes? Sometimes I locate an equivalent from a place like Sears that does classics for another reason—because they're sturdy, and men tend to find them familiarly appealing. But more often I hunt the sale racks at major department stores and other places where bargains are to be had. The jacket I'm wearing in the picture was on a markdown rack in Macy's "Polo" shop. There was a slight gap in one of the inseams. It was reduced from $65 to $19.00, and was this season's Polo, although for something classic it really wouldn't matter to me what season it was.

When I don't see a sale in one of these fancy department store boutique shops, I ask if there's anything damaged in the stock room. I get window display stuff with pin marks or creases that they couldn't get rid of without washing. You have to hit it off with sales clerks to really get a bargain this way, because they usually have to get permission from the manager to mark something down. I ask politely and it usually works: "Have you got anything left over in your stock room from a window display?" Usually they're not at all surprised by the request.

I also like to check out vintage clothing and next-to-new. The rayon shirt I'm wearing in the picture I got at a vintage clothing store for $4.99. I could have gotten a new one, but I happened to like the design and the tailoring was better in those days. The khakis I'm wearing are Calvin Klein's, purchased at one of the end-of-summer sales for $20—half price—in a large men's specialty store. I didn't get much use out of them until the next spring, but then I had new pants that cost much less than the virtually identical new shipment of khakis from that designer.

My white buckskin shoes will never go out of fashion either, and I found them brand new for $12 at a charity bazaar. They probably were brought there by a department store that needed to get rid of leftover stuff.

I guess I do have a general shopping philosophy, which goes something like this: I like clothes, I like to look good, and I don't want to spend everything I make on my appearance. I *look* at expensive stuff for ideas, and I want to look

ROBERT'S OUTFIT

White bucks	*$12.00*
Original price	*$70.00*
Calvin Klein khakis	*$19.00*
Original price	*$40.00*
1940s rayon shirt	*$ 8.00*
Calvin Klein jacket	*$20.00*
Original price	*$65.00*

Robert: "I get window display stuff, sometimes with pin marks or creases that they couldn't get rid of without washing. I ask politely."
(Photo by Ebet Roberts)

"expensive" in what I wear. So I look for clothing that fits my budget but is timeless and well-made. Some people say bargain shopping is time-consuming. Well, I don't have that much time. I fit it in every which way. What I have to do is keep in mind what I still need at any given time to complete an outfit—a shirt, an accessory. Usually it takes at least a couple of weeks to get an outfit completely in place, ready to wear. It doesn't bother me that it takes that long, although I know some men just have to do it all on one shopping trip so they don't have to be bothered anymore until the next season. I read those "bargain" columns in magazines and local papers which tell you of good sales coming up. I like to browse at flea markets and I drop in pretty often at off-price stores where you have to keep on coming regularly to find the good stuff. And I sometimes just go to those ritzy shops that are completely out of my financial league, but just during a clearance sale. The sales in those places are usually pretty marvelous. The bottom line is that I enjoy buying something I know isn't going to be in every other man's closet, something different, maybe with a little sense of humor, too.

I'll give you one more story. I got my new leather jacket in season, from a department store. It's a very handsome jacket. When people compliment me, there's a little smirk inside of me bursting to get out. They're probably wearing a full-price jacket. They treat me as a fashion equal, which I am, though I can't afford to be. Depending on who they are, I might let them in on my little secret. Usually they're amazed and shocked. If I had more money, I might splurge on a couple of things—maybe a great accessory—but by and large, the meat and bones of my buying methods would stay the same.

It used to be considered almost unethical to go the discount route. Now it's open season for bargains.

Amelia: Actress and Mother

I have to keep my ears open to find out about the kinds of clothing I prefer—old stuff, good old stuff. I like the older fabrics—cotton and linen hang better after you've had them a while—and I like the old, pale colors. Also the clothing just seems more *interesting* to me to look at. I just don't want to wear the same thing as anybody else.

The velvet-collared dress I'm wearing in the picture is a case in point. An old woman in my neighborhood, who had been a lawyer, died, and I heard via the grapevine that she had some very well-preserved dresses that had been designed and sewn for her. I was able to take a look. She was just my size and I bought the dress for $18. It was soft, pretty, and it had the over-jacket, which meant the dress could be worn in the spring and fall with the jacket, and in the summer without it.

I bought my suede mini-skirt, which is a deep forest-green color, in a store that sells a combination of jean-type clothing inside that is all new, and has bins outside with a weird assortment of used clothing and outerwear. It is always an adventure, to say the least, to pore over bins like that. The skirt was $3 and appears to be handmade. There was a little stain near the hem in the back, but suede makes its own peculiar marks when you brush it, and unless you really inspected the skirt you'd never notice it. I got the formal jacket I match it up to in a secondhand shop in Denver—it's part of a woman's tuxedo. I feel very historical when I wear it.

I am never attracted to expensive designer clothes that everybody else craves, though I do look at and read about them because I'm interested in fashion. I just don't like being compartmentalized with a million other women who decide to buy some current designer's trendy little blouse. But I do have one secret indulgence of my own. I never buy cheap shoes, or shoes on sale. I buy really expensive shoes, stupidly expensive shoes, and I have no idea why.

When I get a really good bargain, though, I just *know* it's right. I feel that once again I've done something right. Sometimes I even feel thrilled, like when a friend of mine took me to look at a basement filled with untouched, unworn Fifties clothes that somebody had put away after a fire had very slightly damaged them with water. A lot of it was totally fine. There were packets of kids' Davey Crockett shirts and little thin bow ties in the most garish purples and pinks—which would be considered the height of "punk" fashion today—plus dresses, trousers and cotton socks. It wasn't expensive stuff but it was *real* and untouched by time. I bought my son some of these gems.

When I was growing up, our house was always the collection point for church rummage sales. My mother used to say to other parishioners, "You need somewhere to store it? Bring it by." Then, the pair of us would pore over the stuff like hawks. If something was "complete," as my mother called it—a sweater with no holes in it, no matter how horrible it was—she would say, "You can wear this! Go ahead. Put it on." There was wonder in her face. I would say, "I hate it, Mom." She would answer, "But there's nothing *wrong* with it."

I would also wear hand-me-downs from my cousin who was one of those little girls with nice hair and a cute figure. I was fat and had horrible hair and never looked good in her clothes. But I had to take them because they were "complete" —had no holes in them. The rummage stuff was actually much better.

When I was about 12, I began to strike back. I vividly remember taking this table cloth underpad meant for a rummage sale and making a hole in the middle for my head. I thought, "This is it!" I was making my first fashion statement, however odd.

The bargains I get today are an outgrowth of this yearning to be different, I guess. People seem to respond to me better, so I feel more powerful when I look good in an outfit I've put together from bins. If people say, "I like what you're wearing," even if I'm out of work or in a strange place it makes me feel more assertive. And I like it just as well when my six-year-old son goes to the bins or the rummage sales with me and picks out stuff that's different and cute and unusual.

AMELIA'S OUTFIT

Vintage dress	$18.00
Heels	$30.00
Original price	$60.00

Amelia: "When I get a really good bargain I just feel that I've done something cosmically right....Just put me in a Salvation Army store. In between the moldy polyesters there are the rare cottons and linens and laces." (Photo by Ebet Roberts)

I think bargains are the only way to go, now, whether they be old or new. With me, it's old. Just put me in a Volunteers of America or Salvation Army store. There's a lot of junk to be had, but in between the moldy polyesters are the rare cottons and linens and laces. It's really quite wonderful, and when you get to the cash register with that marvelous one-of-a-kind thing you've found, and you know it would cost tons if some new designer came out with it, it comes to 75 cents, maybe. And if you have to stitch it a bit here or there, change the buttons, so much the better. It's a way to get closer to the clothes, and to the people who wore them.

Ann: Public Relations Account Executive

My mother taught me to look for bargains. We made bi-annual trips to Loehmann's in Brooklyn, N.Y., especially for expensive items like coats. A lot of people aren't accustomed to shopping in big bargain places and never feel comfortable about it, but I have developed an "eye" in these places. It doesn't take very much time for me to spot a true bargain.

I can go in, flip through the racks and find the good stuff without necessarily seeing the tags. I'm so good at it that people have stopped to ask me if I am a buyer for the business. I have a scientific method for assessing the clothes. I check for fabric content, look at button holes, how the garment's finished.

My favorite kind of bargain shopping is what I call bulk buying. I make a trip to a bargain place and buy three sweaters, three skirts, a couple of dresses, belts and other accessories—my whole wardrobe for a season in one shot. Sometimes I'll go with friends, and they'll tell me they can't find a thing.

The difference between my mother's bargain attitude and my own is that she can't resist *any* bargain, even if it's *no* bargain at all, not appropriate for anything. She figures she can decide what to do with it later, or at the very worst give it away.

We always argue about this. I believe that's no way to save money—it's a way of spending it unnecessarily, wasting it.

I'm really a shopping meanderer most of the time—rarely buying, always looking. I go to the racks in the back with last season's remains. I often find myself buying these leftovers that have apparently been rejected by others. I like them because they're often high style, dramatic and off-beat, and with my height I can wear clothes like that. And it doesn't bother me that nobody else bought it, because I rely on my own instincts, not just the trend.

What really bothers me today is that expensive clothes are increasingly made from synthetic fabrics. Something "just like silk" is $150. Well, at that price it should be silk. It seems to be an example of the degeneration of quality which designers are capitalizing on. My bargains tend to have lovely fabrics that wear well and breathe well.

This year one of my best purchases was a black, sweatshirty cotton-blend skirt and top which I found at an off-price boutique at the end of the season, but it's really for every season except summer. The outfit cost me $20—it was $60 originally—and seemed to me to have both simplicity and style. It was from a mini-designer who had modified the "Flashdance" design. It also had a Norma Kamali look, very sporty, but it could be worn with heels. The skirt had snaps down the side that gave it a classy look, and, since it was black, it has come in handy as an extra with other tops. Recognizing a good designer imitation is important for a bargain hunter.

I admit to being very aware of labels, but I pride myself in knowing the ones which are well made and also accessible to me economically, like Finity, Carol Horn, Fenn Wright and Mason, designers who are consistently appealing. I couldn't resist the Norma Kamali jumpsuit you see in the picture. My favorite suit and dress are from Kamali, all bought on sale. When I saw the jumpsuit on sale for $9.99 from $100 I

ANN'S OUTFIT

Norma Kamali Jumpsuit	$ 9.99
Original price	$100.00
Sneakers	$ 6.99
Original price	$ 10.99
Patent Leather Belt,	
with Snakeskin Buckle	$ 20.00
Original price	$ 50.00

Ann: "I often find myself buying leftovers that have been rejected by others. I like them because they're often high style, dramatic and off-beat. It doesn't bother me that nobody else has bought it, I rely on my own instincts not just the trend." (Photo by Ebet Roberts) couldn't believe it. My sister, who is not generally a bargain hunter, had bought it earlier in the season for $100. The big shoulder pads made it trendy and perhaps not wearable forever, but the shape is very sensible, with a small waist, and exemplifies Kamali's ability to make her unusual designs applicable to every day. It's 100 percent cotton flannel and an incredible bargain.

Last year I shopped at Bergdorf-Goodman twice—at the end of summer and the end of winter sales—and did incredibly well bargain-wise. Bergdorf doesn't broadcast the exact nature of these sales—you have to know about them to go at the right time. The store puts huge racks in the middle of the floor filled with irresistible bargains like the Angelo Tarlazzi spring/fall coat, marked down from $400 to $130. To me it's as much a bargain as the $9.99 jumpsuit, to get a gorgeous coat from a top designer, a high-style classic that always brings me compliments on it's beautiful soft wool that feels like cashmere, the graceful shoulder pads and pretty buttons.

I think the ritzy department stores are the places to find the best sales on "evergreens," the clothes you'll have and love forever, but I rarely shop in average department stores, even when they have good sales. I just hate having to take only three garments into the dressing room at a time!

***

These comments, from people I believe to be first-rank bargain hunters, unafraid to go after the apparel they want and keenly aware of their own style sense, suggest the wide range of avenues you can travel along the way to *bargain chic*. You can have similar experiences, wherever you live, however much money you have to stock a wardrobe—and enjoy it all as much as Deborah, Robert, Amelia and Ann.

CHAPTER 17

A Real Bargain: What It Is and What It Isn't

INVENTORY CLEARANCE EVENT. ASSISTANT MAN-
AGERS' SALE. PRESIDENTS' BIRTHDAY SALE. TWO-
FOR-ONE SALE. THREE-FOR-TWO SALE. STOCKUP
SALE. MOTHER'S DAY SALE. APRIL FOOL SALES
EVENT. NINE TO MIDNIGHT ONLY SALE. LIQUIDA-
TION SALE. FIRE SALE. UNDER NEW MANAGEMENT
SALE. OUR GREAT HALF-YEARLY SALE. ANNIVER-
SARY SALE EVENT. SUPERSAVERS SALE. 20%–70% OFF
SALE-A-THON. SALE OF A LIFETIME. SALE OF THE
CENTURY. THREE DAYS ONLY BARE-TO-THE-WALLS
BARGAIN BINGE. SUMMER FUN SALE BONANZA.
FEBRUARY WHITE STORE-WIDE CELEBRATION.
GOING-BACK-TO-SCHOOL SPECIAL SALE. PRE-HOLI-
DAY SALE. POST-HOLIDAY BARGAIN BASH. GOING-
OUT-OF-BUSINESS SALE. THE SALE OF SALES. BIG-
GEST SALE IN OUR HISTORY. CENTENNIAL SALE
EVENT. THE BIGGEST SALE WE'VE EVER HAD
SALE . . . and on and on. A sale is a sale is a sale.

"Sales are getting more honest," maintains Iris Ellis, editor
of the *Save On Shopping Directory*, "largely because consumers
are getting smarter, more assertive and more aggressive. They're
willing to hold out for what *they* want in a sale, to get it at the price
they want, rather than to rush in immediately and pay full price.

That's because bargain shoppers ask themselves a very practical question: *Do I want it bad enough to pay full price?* Usually they find they don't, and the fact that they can wait has had great impact on stores. Sometimes, since there are so many sales so often these days, they can get it as early as they need, and at a discount. When I see a 50-percent-off sign, I'm immediately interested. Otherwise, I hold out. So many people are doing this that the stigma of bargain shopping is a thing of the past."

***

Twenty-nine year old Frances owns her own condominium and holds an important position in the computer operations at a large communications corporation.

Despite the upward trajectory of her career, Frances continues to love—and live for—fashion bargains. "More than ever," she effuses at an informal "bargain roundtable" I arranged recently, "they inspire me. When I locate a really sensational buy, I feel powerful, in control. It doesn't matter how much money I make. I still get a tremendous kick out of being 'the one' to discover a good thing. I have no intention of ever outgrowing this habit, no matter how successful I become.

"It was all I could do to keep from gasping," Frances told me of one of her most recent marvelous bargains. "There was a wild look in my eyes, a giddy sensation in my gut. I was literally in a trance. I got the dress, a Ralph Lauren retailing for $350—I saw it at Saks for that—but I paid $95 in a Chicago off-price store."

A native of western New York, Frances lived for many years in Hawaii, and now resides and works in New Jersey. She often travels to her company's home office in Chicago. Wherever she is, Frances knows how to spot a bargain and size it up. If it "fits," in every sense of the word—

- Flatteringly on her figure.
- With apparel already in her wardrobe.

• Into her $150 a month clothing allotment (she's so good at spotting bargains that it need not be higher).

And if the "idea" of it titillates her discerning veteran bargain maven's psyche, only then does Frances seize the moment, pluck the garment from the hanger or the mound, clutch it to her bosom, and gloat. At the cash register, and for many years to come with each compliment received, she'll revel in a glory reserved for the successful bargain hunters and huntresses of the world.

"I can remember every single fashion bargain I ever found," confides Frances. "And I'm always disappointed when I hear about other men and women who can't get it together to participate in what I consider to be this country's great underground sport. Bargain hunting is a high."

Indeed, in the absence of pirate's gold, sniffing out bargains to decorate our bodies can be a modern-day treasure hunt. Piecing together the clues demands a finely tuned combination of instinct and science.

The aims of the discount detective are simple and, hopefully, guilt-free:

• to outwit competitors (other shoppers, stores and manufacturers).
• to satisfy inner cravings of ownership.
• to look great or stretch our wallets—or why not both?
• to have the last consumer laugh in an era of spiraling inflation.

Our apologies to hard-working retailers trying to make a buck, but in this every-man-and-woman-for-himself society, making any kind of individual statement separates us from the drones and followers and other don't-rock-the-boat types. A typical fashion bargain, for example, a pair of I. Miller patent leather pumps gobbled up recently for $30 in an off-price show haven, down 50 percent from Miller's own stores, may seem like a small victory to those who have always eschewed bargains. But the aim of knowing how to shop wisely on a shoestring, and yet to look like the most terrific person on your block, has always had plenty of quiet adherents.

Designer Willi Smith says it succinctly: "You don't have to go broke if you are trying to be fashionable."

There's no denying the many levels of value. A $500 dress that looks like a million and is worn that many times is exceptionally valuable, even if one pays $500 for it. But so is a $50 dress reduced to $9.99—if it is purchased by the right person at the right time. The simple truth is that the sale racks of America are filled with the best buys in America stocked by the best designers in America.

The most fashionable apparel for men and women is available at prices nobody can believe. The old battle cry of the full-price crowd has always been that "nothing on sale ever looks right on me." Listen to the comments of Neil, who was raised on Bloomingdale's and Brooks Brothers.

"My father took us to each of these stores once a year for pants and sport jackets. We had just enough to get by—who could have two of anything at those prices?—but I had those jackets for 15 years. Sale? That was a sub-species. It wasn't until I got married to a bargain genius that I discovered the bottomless pit of value you could find practically everywhere. I got my first leather jacket in Syms in 1974, reduced from $300 to $88. I realized I could have more clothing, including items like the leather jacket, which I never could have afforded at retail. The Italian cotton/linen shirts that were my trademark in the late 1970s were reduced from $35 each to $3.99 in Abraham & Straus. I'm not even afraid to try out a so-called 'schlock' store that doesn't seem at first glance to be my kind of place. The funny thing—no, the wonderful thing—is that I have found great value in these stores, too. I bought a winter coat a few years ago that was obviously a designer rip-off cut. It was $59. Okay, so it wasn't the 'real thing.' But people didn't know. I got compliments on it until it was finally put to rest after five years. And now that I'm out in the corporate world, I go to NBO for suits, and they're Harris tweeds and delicate wools from the best designers—at about half the cost of the pricey stores. Now I even brag to my wife about my bargains. I would feel as if I were a traitor to the cause if I didn't get my clothes at the best possible price."

Frances and Neil have more in common than their ability to scout sale racks. They've used bargain hunting to create a personal style made up of equal parts of sophistication, practicality, comfort and value.

For them, shopping has become more than the the proverbial dull necessity because there's nothing more enjoyable than *finding* that bargain in the rough.

Competing in the fashion bargain free-for-all depends not only on personal style and instinct but on knowledge of the modus operandi of stores of all kinds, and that every item has two, three or even more prices at which it is readily available. Once you know where and how to spot a bargain or sashay to a sale staged by stores now open seven days a week in many areas, you'll be on your way.

"A lot of people are empty-headed when they shop," muses West Coast bargain hunter, Viki King. "They do it purely as an amusement, even when spending large sums of money. But the fact is that it's a business. If you do it right, if you don't throw your money away, if you find clothes that enhance you and you put those bargains together smartly, it's an investment too."

I would add it's also the key to *bargain chic.*

The Bargain Chic Fashion Resource Shopping Guide

The following list, reflecting subjective shoppers' impressions, was compiled with the help of fashion and lifestyle editors from major newspapers in the cities listed below. Stores included in this resource guide offer either regular markdowns of at least 50 percent off original retail of first quality branded merchandise, or regular sales worth knowing about. Stores are identified according to type and are listed in alphabetical order.

Code used for store type:
Boutique (B)
Department Store (DS)
Discount Department Store (DC)
Kids (K)
Men's Specialty (MS)
Off-Price (OP)
Outlet (O)
Resale (R)
Shoes (SH)
Vintage/Second Hand (V)
Women's Specialty (WS)

***

Atlanta
Burlington Coat Factory (OP)
Loehmann's (OP)

NBO (MS/OP)
Play It Again, Sam (V)
Puttin' On The Ritz (V)
Rich's (DS)
Stefan (V)

Baltimore
Anders Clothing Clearance
Center (MS/OP)
Apparel Associates (O)
Bamberger's (DS)
Bata Factory Store (SH)
Burlington Coat Factory (OP)
C-Mart (DC)
Clothes Closet (V)
Donlevy's Backroom (OP)
The Handbag Place (SH)
Hutzler's (DS)
Jos. A. Bank Clothiers (MS/
WS/OP)
Loehmann's (OP)
NBO (MS/OP)

Boston
Ann Taylor Warehouse (O)
Bertha Cool (V)
Burlington Coat Factory (OP)
Filenes (OP)
Jordan Marsh (DS)
Loehmann's (OP)
NBO (MS/OP)
Silver Threads (V)

Charlotte, NC
Ivey's (DS)
Junior League Shop (V)
Mechlenberg Flea Market (V)
Montaldo's (MS/WS)

T. Edwards (B)
T.J. Maxx (OP)

Chicago
Baskin's (MS/WS)
Benjamin's (MS)
Brigsby and Kruthers (MS)
Brittany Ltd. (MS)
Burlington Coat Factory (OP)
Carson Pirie Scott (DS)
Handmoor (OP)
Mallards (MS)
Mark Shale (MS/WS)
Marshall Field (DS)
NBS (MS/OP)
Zuggurat (V)

Cincinnati
Anders (OP)
Burlington Coat Factory (OP)
Chatterlings (OP)
Downtown (V)
Gentry Shops (MS)
Hit or Miss (OP)
Marshalls (OP)
Potter Shoe Outlet (SH)
Shoe Market (SH)
Terri Lee's Show Room (WS/OP)
T.H. Mandy (OP)
T.J. Maxx (OP)

Columbus
Burlington Coat Factory (OP)
Lazarus (DS)
The Limited (OP)
NBO (MS/OP)
Newmarket (OM)

Schottenstein's (OP)
Unicorn (V)

Dallas
Ahab Bowen (V/SH)
Apparel Mart (OP)
Bloomingdale's (DS)
Burlington Coat Factory (OP)
Clothes Horse Anonymous (R/MS/WS)
Flaunt (V)
The Limited (OP)
Loehmann's (OP)
Timothy's (SH)

Denver
Auers (B)
Burlington Coat Factory (OP)
The Denver (DS)
Designer 3 (OP)
Loehmann's (OP)
The Ritz (V)
Woolrich (O)

Detroit
Backstage Affair (V)
Burlington Coat Factory (OP)
Designer Depot (DC)
Esther & Estelle (B)
Fabulous Second Hand (V)
Hattie Inc. (B)
Hit or Miss (OP)
Hudson's (DS)
J.C. Penney (DS)
Jacobson's (WS/MS)
The Limited (OP)
Linda Dresner (B)
Marshalls (OP)
Patti Smith's (V)

Ray and Ida (B)
Roz and Sherm (B)
Sachs (DS)
T. J. Maxx (OP)

Houston
Burlington Coat Factory (OP)
Flashbacks (V)
Foley's (DS)
Joseph A. Banks (MS)
Macy's (DS)
T.H. Mandy (OP)

Indianapolis
Burlington Coat Factory (OP)
Donlevy's Backroom (OP)
J.C. Penney (DS)
L.L. Ayres (DS)
Loehmann's (OP)
McGuire's Gazebo (B)
Modern Times (V)
T.J. Maxx (OP)
Value City (DC)

Kansas City, MO
Anders (MS/OP)
Coat Outlet (OP)
Dress Racque (OP)
Marshalls (OP)

Los Angeles
Apparel Warehouse (OP)
Bulloch's (DS)
C and R Clothiers (MS/OP)
Cecil Elrod (B)
Continuations (V)
Cooper Building (OP)
Dimensions (OP)

Foster's (SH/M&W)
Growing Tree (K/R)
Happy Millionaire (MS/WS/B)
Importique (B)
In Skin (WS/MS-Outerwear)
Jack and Jill (K)
Kidsmart (K)
Labels (V)
Loehmann's (OP)
Orbachs (DS)
Pumpkin Patch (K/R)
Right Bank Shoes (SH)
Robinson's (DS)
Roger Stuart's (MS)
Ross Stores (OP)
Sacks SFO (OP)
Samples Only (SH)
1717 Outlet (O/M)
Shoes by Shirley (SH)
Steven Craig (MS)

Encino
La Rue Clothes of Yesteryear
(V)

Pasadena
Clothes Heaven (V)
Gentleman's Agreement (V)
The Ritz (V)
Silent Partners (V)

Memphis
Burlington Coat Factory (OP)
Eugenia's (V)
Goldsmith's (DS)
Loehmann's (OP)
The Show Room (OP)
SteinMart (OP)

Miami
Bonwit Teller (DS)
Burdine's (DS)
Empire (OP)
Loehmann's (OP)
Macy's (DS)
Martha (B)
Syms (OP)
24 Collection (B)

Milwaukee
Branovan Outlet Store (M/OP)
Burlington Coat Factory (OP)
Clothes Rack (O)
Florence Eiseman (B)
Half-Price Shoe Outlet (SH)
Hit or Miss (OP)
Jeans Sample Shop (B)
Loehmann's (OP)
Sizes Unlimited (OP)
Sweet Doomed Angel (V)
Trendsetter Fashions (OP)

Minneapolis
Connco (SH)
Dayton's (DS)
Ed Holmberg (WS)
R.D. Minquist (B)
Ragstock (V)

New York City (NY)/Brooklyn (Br), Long Island (LI), Queens (Q)
Aaron's (Br) (OP)
Abraham and Straus (Br) (DS)
Alexander's (NY/Br/LI/Q) (DS)
Berta (Br) (B)
Big Deal$ (NY/O)

Bloomingdale's (NY) (DS)
Bolton's (NY/LI) (OP)
Bubba's Way (NY) (R)
Burlington Coat Factory (LI) (OP)
C and C Bargains (BR) (K)
Chuckles (NY) (OP)
Clothes-Out (LI) (OP)
Conway (NY) (K)
Council Thrift Shop (NY) (V)
Discount Fashions (Br) (OP)
Dollar Bill's (NY) (MS/OP)
Emotional Outlet (NY) (OP)
Empire (NY/LI) (OP)
Filene's (LI) (OP)
Gap Manhattan Clearance Ctr. (NY)
Girl's Club Thrift Shop (NY) (V)
Gwenda D. (NY) (V)
Joyce Leslie (NY/Br) (OP)
Lewis & Clark (NY) (MS/OP)
Loehmann's (BR/LI/Q) (OP)
Lupu's (Br) (OP)
Macy's (NY/Q) (DS)
Merns (NY) (MS/OP)
Natan Borlam (Br) (K)
NBO (NY/Q) (M/OP)
The New Store (NY) (OP)
Odd Job Trading (NY) (O)
Odd Lot Trading (NY) (O)
Orbach's (NY/LI) (DS)
Plymouth Shops (NY/LI) (DS)
S & W Outlet (NY) (OP/O)
Strawberry (NY/Br) (OP)
Syms (NY) (OP)
TSS/Seedman's (LI) (DC)
Weber's Clearance Centers
(NY) (O)
Zoom (NY) (O)

Paramus, NJ
Bolton's (WS/OP)
Burlington Coat Factory (OP)
Daffy Dan's (OP)

Philadelphia
Brownie's Sportswear (OP)
Burlington Coat Factory (OP)
Dry Goods (OP)
Golden Harry's Bargains (OP)
Jos. A. Bank Clothiers (OP)
M & S Shoes (SH)
My Sister's Place (B/OP)
Supreme Merchandise Co. (OP)
A Touch of Panache (V)
Wanamaker's (DS)

Pittsburgh
Alexander's (OP)
Anders (MS/OP)
Anonymous (V)
Burlington Coat Factory (OP)
Gimbels (DS)
Horne's (DS)
Kaufmann's (DS)
Loehmann's (OP)
Name Dropper (V)
Second Time Around (V)
Specialty Clothing (MS/OP)
T.J. Maxx (OP)
The Vamp (V)

Portland, OR
Loehmann's (OP)
Meier and Frank (DS)
Mercantile (B)
One More Time (V)

Rochester, NY
Burlington Coat Factory (OP)
Champion (O)
Cohoes (OP)
Donlevy's Backroom (OP)
Gold Circle (DC)
K-Mart (DC)
Marshalls (OP)
McCurdy's (DS)
Peter Harris (OP)

St. Louis
Dillards (DS)
Fashion Barn (OP)
The Limited (OP)
Marshalls (OP)
Nostalgia (V)
The Right Price (OP)
Sachs (DS)

San Francisco
Donna Piller's (B/SH)
Esprit de Corps (O)
Loehmann's (OP)
Matinee (V)
Macy's (DS)
Marshalls (OP)

Seattle
Anders (MS/OP)
Coats, Etc. (OL)
Delux Junk (V)
Factory Fallout (OP)
Frederick and Nelson (DS)
Fritzi Ritz (V)
Jeans Warehouse (O)
Loehmann's (OP)
Seattle Trade Center (O)

Washington, DC/Virginia (Va)
Bloomingdale's (Va) (DS)
Burlington Coat Factory (Va)
(OP)
Children's Wear Market (Va)
(OP)
Gentlemen's Wear-House (Va)
(OP)
Lord and Taylor (DS)
Marshalls (OP)
NBO (DC/Va) (OP)
Second Hand Rose (Va) (V)
Syms (Va) (OP)
T.H. Mandy (OP)
Wall Street Clothes (Va) (MS/
OP)
Woodward and Lothrop (DS)

Major Outlet Centers and Malls

(Source: SOS Inc./and their publication, the *Save on Shopping Directory*)

Boaz, Alabama
Los Angeles, Ca.
Hartford, Ct.
Norwalk, Ct.
Altamonte Springs, Fla.
Clearwater, Fla.
Daytona, Fla.
Miami, Fla.
Orlando, Fla.
Talahassee, Fla.
Tampa, Fla.
Atlanta, Ga.
Duluth, Ga.
Marietta, Ga.
Ringgold, Ga.

Rossville, Ga.
Valdosta, Ga.

Chicago, Ill.
Downer's Grove, Ill.
Rockford, Ill.
Indianapolis, Ind.
Merrillville, Ind.
Nishawaka, Ind.
Davenport, Iowa
Des Moines, Iowa
Louisville, Ky.
Shreveport, La.
Elsworth, Me.
Freeport, Me.
Kittery, Me.
Wells Corner, Me.

Gaithersburg, Md.
Greenbelt, Md.
Jessup, Md.
Fall River, Mass.
North Dartmouth, Mass.
New Bedford, Mass.
Ann Arbor, Mich.
Farmington, Mich.
Farmington Hills, Mich.
Grand Rapids, Mich.
Muskegon, Mich.
Rochester, Mich.
Rockford, Mich.
Traverse City, Mich.
Eden Prairie, Minn.
Oakdale, Minn.
Red Wing, Minn.
Wentzville, Mo.
Conway, N.H.

Manchester, N.H.
Nashua, N.H.
North Conway, N.H.
Northhampton, N.H.
Portsmouth, N.H.

Fairfield, N.J.
Flemington, N.J.
Matawan, N.J.
Secaucus, N.J.
Carle Place, N.J.
Colonie, N.Y.
Greece, N.Y.
Monticello, N.Y.
Mt. Kisco, N.Y.
Niagara Falls, N.Y.
Ogdensburg, N.Y.
Penfield, N.Y.
Rochester, N.Y.
Syracuse, N.Y.
Utica, N.Y.
West Seneca, N.Y.

Burlington, N.C.
Charlotte, N.C.
Greensboro, N.C.
Kannapolis, N.C.
Morrisville, N.C.
Raleigh, N.C.
Winston-Salem, N.C.
Fargo, N.D.
Kings Island, Ohio
Moore, Okla.
Oklahoma City, Okla.
Tulsa, Okla.
Erie, Pa.

Lancaster, Pa.
Redding, Pa.
Waynesboro, Pa.
York, Pa.
Charleston, S.C.
Columbia, S.C.
Greenville, S.C.
Myrtle Beach, S.C.
Spartanburg, S.C.
Goodlettsville, Tenn.
Knoxville, Tenn.
Lakeland, Tenn.
Murphysboro, Tenn.
Pigeon Forge, Tenn.

Allen, Texas
Austin, Texas
El Paso, Texas
Houston, Texas
Mesquite, Texas
N. Richland Hills, Texas
Brattleboro, Vt.
South Burlington, Vt.

Fairfax, Va.
Lightfoot, Va.
Norfolk, Va.
Roanoke, Va.
Virginia Beach, Va.
Tukwila, Washington
Martinsburg, W. Va.
Green Bay, Wisc.
Kenosha, Wisc.
LaCrosse, Wisc.
Madison, Wisc.
Clover, Wisc.
West Bend, Wisc.

The SOS Save on Shopping Directory, Villard Books, $10.95, is available in bookstores everywhere. For more information on outlet centers and malls throughout the U.S.A., write SOS, Inc., 9109 San Jose Blvd., Jacksonville, Fl 32217, or call 1-904-733-8877.

Major Off-Price Children's Clothing Chain Stores

Check your local yellow pages for the addresses of these highly regarded off-price clothing chains that offer children's clothing.

Burlington Coat Factory
Children's Outlet
Children's Wearhouse
Childrenswear Outlet
Carter's Factory Outlet
Champion Factory Outlet
Fabulous Julie's
Fashion Flair
Filene's
Front Row
House of Bargains
Jamboree
Just Kids
Kids Port U.S.A.
Kids 'R' Us
Kidswear Stores
Lincoln Factory Outlet
The Kids Stop
J. Brannum
Jumping Jack's Shoes
Marlowe Kids
Marshalls
N.B.C.
Peter Harris
Polly Flinder's Factory Outlet
T.J. Maxx
Quoddy Factory Shoe Outlet
Ross Stores
Sweaterville
Tultex Apparel Mill Outlet

Top 20 Department Stores

Macy's New York
Bamberger's New Jersey
Macy's California
The Broadway, S. California
Dillard's, Little Rock
Bloomingdale's, New York
Abraham & Straus, Brooklyn
Hudson's, Detroit
May, California
Marshall Field, Chicago
Lord and Taylor, New York
Burdine's, Miami
Foley's, Houston
Bullock's, S. California
Emporium Capwell, San Francisco
Dayton's, Minnesota
Rich's, Atlanta
Hecht, Washington, D.C.
Jordan Marsh, New England
Lazarus, Columbus

SOURCE: *Chain Store Age* (1983 statistics).

Top 15 Chain Retailers

Sears
K-Mart
J.C. Penney
Federated:
  Bloomingdale's
  Abraham & Straus
  Burdine's
  Foley's
  Gold Circle
  Bullock's
  Rich's
  Lazarus

Richway
Filene's
The Children's Place
Levy's
Dayton Hudson
   Target
   Mervyn's
   Hudson's
   Dayton's
Montgomery Ward
F.W. Woolworth
Wal-Mart
May Dept. Stores
   Venture
   May
   Hecht
   Famous Barr
   Volume Shoe
   Kaufmann's
   Meier & Frank
Associated Dry Goods
   Caldor
   Lord and Taylor
   J.W. Robinson
   Loehmann's
   L.S. Ayers
   Sibley
   Horne
   Denver Dry Goods
   Hahne
   Goldwater's
   Robinson's
   Stewart's
   Powers
Allied Stores
   Jordan Marsh
   The Bon
   Stern's
   Mass Bros.

Brooks Bros.
Pomeroy's
Bonwit Teller
Garfinkel's
Carter Hawley Hale
Broadway
Emporium Capwell
Neiman-Marcus
John Wanamaker's
Weinstock's
Thalheimer
Holt Renfrew
R.H. Macy
Bamberger's
Macy's
Davison's
Melville Corp.
Batus
Saks
Marshall Field
Gimbels
Frederick & Nelson
Kohl's

SOURCE: *Chain Store Age* (1983 statistics).

Remember, it's always better if the price is right. (Photo by Joan Tedeschi)

Bargain Chic Glossary

AS IS—Rips, non-functional zipper, missing buttons, lipstick stain. Something happened to this item after it got to the store and you're buying it on the cheap because of it.

CLEARANCE—Merchandise has been on the floor too long and it's literally being "cleared out."

COMPARABLE VALUE—The inherent value of the merchandise is about the same as branded goods that should cost more.

IRREGULARS—Clothing is marred by slight imperfections in fabric, size, pattern, ornamentation. Problems are often difficult to spot, though, without a magnifying glass or X-ray vision. By law, manufacturer must stamp "IRREGULAR" across the label if it is.

LIQUIDATION—A store is closing its doors forever and the merchandise must be sold. (*Warning:* Some stores use this word to attract customers but have no intention either of giving you a bargain or going out of business.)

OVERSTOCK—The manufacturer made too much, or else was stuck with a store's last-minute cancellation of an order. This apparel is often in mint condition and of up-to-the-minute fashion timeliness, but sells for less, most likely in an off-price or outlet venue.

SECONDS—Apparel has fairly obvious defects in workmanship or materials. Look for arrows or dots pasted to clothing at the point of imperfection.

SPECIAL PURCHASE—Merchandise acquired solely for the purpose of offering it on sale. It may *not* necessarily reflect the usual quality of the store.